# WORK FINDING

## BILL GREGORY

BOOK PUBLISHERS NETWORK

Book Publishers Network
P.O. Box 2256
Bothell • WA • 98041
PH • 425-483-3040
www.bookpublishersnetwork.com

10 9 8 7 6 5 4 3 2 1

Printed in the United States of America

LCCN  2010934498
ISBN10  1-935359-58-4
ISBN13  978-1-935359-58-6

*Editor: Julie Scandora*
*Cover Designer: Laura Zugzda*
*Typographer: Stephanie Martindale*

Photo credits:
pp 1 © Michael Dykstra | Dreamstime.com, pp 5 © Freelion Wu | Dreamstime.com, pp 37 © Farzin Salimi | Dreamstime.com, pp i, 63, 127, 243, 261 © Jan Martin Will | Dreamstime.com, pp 87, 121, 181 © Le Do | Dreamstime.com, pp 101 © Phant | Dreamstime.com, pp 117, 217 © Nina Morozova | Dreamstime.com, pp 191 © Noel Powell | Dreamstime.com, pp 203 © Photka | Dreamstime.com, pp 237 © Kaspri | Dreamstime.com, pp 255 © Juliengrondin | Dreamstime.com

# A Labyrinth and Your Work Finding Path

The cover image is a labyrinth in a public park on the Island of Cres, just off the Croatian Adriatic coast. It was designed by Goran Susic and installed in 1994. It is similar in design and purpose to the labyrinth on the floor of the cathedral at Chartres, mandalas from eastern religions, and the medicine wheel from the Native American tradition. The thousands of people each year who walk labyrinths located in spiritual and physical health centers throughout the world report a feeling of being centered and increased self-awareness resulting from walking along the concentric circles from the outside towards the center. Applying their experiences to building success in our career, we can picture ourselves on a similar walk. Growing to become better able to be successful in our career begins when we are on the outside path, looking at what is happening in the world around us. On the inner paths, our observation moves inward, about how we are thinking and what we are feeling as we meet life's challenges. As we move closer to the center, we can get insights about our strengths and areas for improvement that stand behind our experiences in the world. At the center, which symbolizes our self, we find the potential to connect to a source of power.

The ideas and activities of *Work Finding* lead you along a growth path to give you the extra punch you need to achieve your career goals. It contains:

- Activities to build a stronger self by recognizing and learning from your accomplishments.

- Suggestions for building capacities that develop your whole person.

- A competency-driven self-assessment process that provides the best possible help for identifying your priority interests and abilities.

- Keys to exploring in ways that will expand your perceptions.

- Examples of how to network in a way that will connect you with the right people and the best opportunities for you.

- A process for identifying and overcoming obstacles and improving your performance.

In both walking a labyrinth and interacting with people about job opportunities, the key is listening, and opening your heart and mind to possibilities.

# CONTENTS

Acknowledgements                                                    vii

   Chapter One: Your Work of Art                                 1

   Chapter Two: Sensing a Stronger Self                          5

   Chapter Three: Career Choice Points                          37

   Chapter Four: Connecting With Competency Stories             63

   Chapter Five: Unique Résumé                                  87

   Chapter Six: Expanding Perceptions                          101

   Chapter Seven: Interacting Through Walking                  117

   Chapter Eight: Interacting Through Paper and
      Computer Screen                                         121

   Chapter Nine: Interacting in Conversations                  127

   Chapter Ten: Internet Social Networking                     181

   Chapter Eleven: Work Finding Persistence                     191

Chapter Twelve: Memorable Interview 203

Chapter Thirteen: Overcoming Obstacles 217

Chapter Fourteen: Balance Over Stress 237

Chapter Fifteen: Building New Competencies 243

Chapter Sixteen: Integrating to Improve Performance 255

Chapter Seventeen: Hearing a Call 261

Appendix I: Ten Coach or Counselor Steps for Facilitating
   Competency Based Interests and Abilities Discovery 267

References 271

About The Author 275

# Acknowledgements

My interactions with my clients, the unique and beautiful people in whose career paths I have participated as a counselor, gave rise to the many specifics about successful career counseling and coaching that appear in *Work Finding*. Thank you all.

I have been fortunate to have been in a student/mentoring/ employee relationship with career development leaders who have influenced my practice of career counseling. Bernard Haldane, who skillfully promoted the importance of recognizing accomplishments and is the distinguished founder of the firm named after him, taught how everyone performs his or her job in a unique way and pioneered ways to discover that. Professor Jerald Forster of the University of Washington explored how people can improve their career from understanding how they construct their reality with their thinking. Cal Crow, Seattle University teacher and consultant, applies compassion and new ideas in helping people to learn about themselves and move forward in their career. Jerry Pipes, head of counseling at Human Resource Associates, characterized networking as spreading the love around, and he lives that message. Bill Levings, principal of Right Management in Seattle, engaged outplacement contracts and counseled in a way that featured listening, helping, and reinforcement. Tom Jackson, well-known author and consultant, creates new ways of understanding and responding to job market dynamics and influences human resource practices in organizations.

Dan Cahn envisioned new aggregations for career Web portals as head of Worklife Solutions, and Melanie Keveles and Bill Pilder provided innovative and insightful career ideas for the Web sites.

The students of Bastyr University, which educates and trains naturopathic doctors, acupuncturists, and nutritionists, inspire by pursuing a life committed to an ideal. Scott Buessing and Will Englehart were especially helpful in testing some of the counseling and healing approaches in the book.

Colleagues at the Puget Sound Career Development Association, such as Mary Lou Hunt, Kay Bell, Jan Reha, Larry Gaffin, Tom Washington, David Roy, Craig Riggs, Allan Hay, and Terry Pile, have always had good ideas about moving things forward.

This book would not have been possible without the capable assistance from the competent professionals at the Book Publishers Network, led by Sheryn Hara. They are Julie Scandora, editing; Laura Zugzda, cover design; and Stephanie Martindale, layout. I would also like to thank Cindy Buffa for her editing and understanding.

I appreciate the loving support of my family. My wife Barbara has made both practical and artistic observations to improve the book. My son John helped with setting a high goal, and daughter Anne contributed an understanding of how to motivate people.

Thank you.

## CHAPTER ONE

# YOUR WORK OF ART

"**W**ow, that is a work of art!"

Have you ever said that to someone about a completed project at work? Has anyone ever said that to you? Or have you ever even thought that about your work? Maybe not. Although you may recognize the importance of your contributions through your job, you might not see their connection to an inspiring career. In your job, you may create an excellent product or service, but you may not feel that the work increases your energy for life. You may see that your job helps your company succeed, but it may not draw on your unique creativity. While your efforts may give value to the customer, you may not feel a motivating personal connection. You may enjoy the monetary reward of your job, but you may feel short-changed in the less tangible benefits from the work. In the end, you may care more about what you will do when you leave for the day than what you are doing while on the job.

If you are in school training for an occupation, you need to have faith that you will find a high interest area that will make your studies fun and rewarding. If you are a new graduate, you may need to trust that the optimism and hope you feel now at the beginning of your career will propel you beyond a possibly limited first job in a new career.. If you have been in a career job for a while and no longer feel zeal, you may need to rekindle the enthusiasm you had at the start.

Over ten years ago author and humanist William Bridges identified the need to move from viewing employment as a mere job to something much greater, a new way of acting, which he termed "work." He called for a "job shift" to eliminate seeing the job as a box that serves an organizational master and to view it as a marketing activity with no boundaries in how the needs of customers both inside of and outside of organizations are viewed.[1] In this definition, work means more than what a person does for a living. It also implies expression of one's self and one's effectiveness in the world.

Tom Jackson, well known for originating tactics that help people to win in the job market, uses the word "work" to describe its essential connection to a good life. "Your work experience is the primary social/economic/spiritual relationship in your life." Jackson emphasizes that personal growth is needed to elevate work to this level in your life. His work includes tactics for overcoming fears and internal resistances, as well as for eliciting help in overcoming shortcomings. Several of the tactics he recommends help people find their best work, not just a job.[2]

We find work rewarding when we express our values, interests, abilities, and preferences. Our whole personality focuses on what we are doing and flows into it so that it becomes an extension of our self. Going to work is seen as an opportunity to create something we can take pride in. And when we succeed at our work, we have created a "work of art." The phrase, "I am going to do my work" usually conveys more involvement and pride than "I am going to do my job."

The relationship successful authors have with their books, musicians with their songs, inventors with their inventions, software developers with their lines of code, and managers with their teams all revolve around passion. Everyone, regardless of education and skills, regardless of chosen occupation, can feel passionate about what he or she does.

Passionately expressing our creativity in work is also a requirement for our economic survival. Popular writer Daniel Pink, in *A Whole New Mind*, shows that the routine parts of our job hold no future for us; they can be done more quickly by automation or more cheaply in Asia.[3] He says that we have moved from the Information Age in which knowledge workers process information to the Conceptual Age requiring creativity and empathy. To succeed, doctors need to hone their skills in observation and empathy because patients can glean medical information from the Internet. Marketing channel workers such as wholesalers and manufacturing reps need to create new approaches because automated supply chains have replaced distribution channels. Accountants and lawyers are still needed for creative insights, but routine accounting and legal work can be performed in Asia at a lower cost. Information technology experts are needed to automate processes in new ways, but writing computer code can be automated or performed less expensively in places such as India.

Most likely, what you are doing now will contribute positively to advancement along your ideal career path. So build upon it! Identify your path more clearly so that what you are doing will be part of a meaningful career future. At this point, passion will naturally enter your working life, making you more enthused to work, in turn making you more effective, spiraling ever upward in your successful career.

This passion will come when you move from "job finding" to "work finding." Job finders scour listings of jobs online, in newspaper classifieds, and in professional journals to identify those for which they possess the requested qualifications. They then write a letter showing how their interests and skills fit the situation and attach their résumé. If they get an interview, they struggle further to portray themselves as the perfect person for the situation. This immense effort has very low odds of success because companies that create job descriptions and list jobs are looking for someone with specific and successful experience in their industry. If it were easy for a person with varied or outside experience to fit in, they would have hired one of the many people who constantly contact the human resource department or one of their current employees.

In work finding, you, the individual, focus on reaching out, based on what your inner voice says you need to do to live a good life. Because all work involves meeting the needs of people on some level, work finding emphasizes interacting with others. In meeting people during a career and work search beginning interactions lead to other possibilities. Your discussions bring out new ideas. Collaborations enrich your options.

All help you move forward. You feel welcome personal improvement as you adapt to new environments. You take on mannerisms that help you fit into a new work culture. You talk the language and connect to part of a network. You unite with your coworkers through a meeting of the minds. You fit in.

In summary,

- A job comes from the outside; work comes from within.

- A job is designed by an employer; work is designed by the finder.

- The rewards of a job are largely money and status; work is its own reward.

- Job finding involves seeing what is required and changing how you think about yourself to be the person an employer, someone else, is looking for. Work finding involves first knowing yourself and then either finding work that fits you, growing internally to fit into more places, or shaping how you see the workplace so that it is an expression of who you are.

In the following chapters, we provide a process that will help you to see jobs, work, career, and your future in a new light. The steps we provide will prepare you for this grand adventure in work finding. Throughout, we will confront questions that have no one correct answer.

In this introduction we have shown the difference between striving for a career with meaning and just doing the minimum to survive in what you see as only a job.

- Do you love your job?

- Do you find meaning in your work beyond the satisfaction of supporting yourself and possibly others?

- Are you performing at a level that will enable you to achieve a work of art?

# Chapter Two

# Sensing a Stronger Self

Many people, when in a career quandary, seek help outside of themselves. They often start by looking for interesting job openings and then progress to reading about occupations that might interest them. Some people get good ideas and act on them. But most give up looking because they fail to identify a strong interest they believe is both realistic and attainable. Some never bother looking and only complain and say, "There is nothing out there for me." The truth is that we won't see anything "out there" until we sense strongly what is "in here," what we hold inside of us. We need to move from liking something because of its currently popularity to liking it because of its connection to our own values, interests, and abilities. In work finding, we must know our self in order to recognize work that will fit our personality and desires. Ask yourself questions—about you, about the events around you, about your feelings. How are you reacting to what is happening in the world? What inspires you? What looks like fun? What would you love to do now?

As children we could easily answer these questions. In those early years, we woke up full of energy and optimism for all of the possible activities for the day. We had very few memories of failures or messages from adults about what we were supposed to do.

Career experts agree that self-understanding is a crucial first step towards career success. "Most job-hunters who fail to find their dream job, fail not because they lack information about the job-market, but because they lack information about themselves."[1]

# INTRINSIC MOTIVATION

A strong self works from intrinsic motivation rather than from outside rewards, whether accolades, monetary compensation, or gold stars. Too often we carry out activities that we think will meet others expectations: instead of understanding what we most care about; we tend to deny our true self rather than setting our performance goals based upon who we really are. Instead of acting on our instincts, we too often mimic what others would do. As a result, we suppress our true nature, toning down a free and full expression of our self, and if done too often, lose a sense of the very essence of our self. Our innately healthy core does not speak sufficiently, and our career moves along without our inner fire. We all want to "be somebody," but too often we try to be somebody by being somebody else.

When we are very young, our survival depends on other people. We learn to do what they say and to please them in order to get what we need. In our adolescent years, we start stretching at the bonds of dependency. We see a difference between the desires of our self and the desires of other people and begin to express an identity that sets us apart from others, nurturing it by elevating certain skills and interests above others. To strengthen further our emerging self, we seek groups— usually apart from the family we still depend upon—that will reinforce what we are becoming.

From this point on, we continually confront the crucial decision: to follow the desires we call our own or to do what other people want us to do. When we act from within, we feel an intrinsic motivation. When we act to please others, we are working with extrinsic motivation, one that seeks rewards from those outside of our self. Many people operate at this level, chasing the latest fad, trying to make others happy, toeing the line when their spirit urges them to break free. They find security in doing what others approve of and gladly relinquish responsibility for making independent decisions. They willingly follow the masses, and if they "choose" wrong, at least they will have lots of company.

But what do they lose in ignoring the voice within? They deny their true self and deep inside they know they are living incompletely. On a grander scale, they are denying the world the benefit of their unique talents and ways of thinking. No one gains, not in the long run, when people suppress their true selves.

But before strengthening our true self, we must first have an awareness of that self. Therefore, we begin by listening more to what is inside of us than to those who are outside of us. This means that we are willing to take some steps which might be risky. Recall a time when you:

- Selected a hobby or activity based on your interests instead of doing something because your friends wanted to do it or because everyone in the family did it.

- When in a discussion, expressed an opinion that you truly believed but might have been unpopular.

- Spent time following a vague hunch.

## WHOLE-SELF DEVELOPMENT

When we look within, what do we see? What is in our awareness, and where do we place our attention? What we find falls into four categories: sensations, feelings, thoughts, and intuitions which come from our physical, emotional, intellectual, and non-physical or spiritual nature. If we close our eyes and identify what is in our awareness in this mode, our physical senses will alert us to sounds, maybe a whiff of some scent, and what we are touching—the carpet, cushions of a chair, material in our clothing. We will feel an emotion such as love or worry. We will have thoughts revolving around conversations just ended, tasks at hand, plans for the future, and much more, all helping us make logical sense of our world. We will have new ideas, gut feelings about possibilities. Carl Jung identified these four themes from his observations of his patients as a psychiatrist, his insights from regular social interactions, and his understanding of himself.[2] He also acknowledged that his research into ancient philosophical literature contributed to his description of how individuals differ from one another. Psychologists still use these themes, which he called "functions," in tests and analyses that help people understand and develop themselves.

The following arrangement is the way humans have always seen themselves, and it is seen in ancient symbols that come from our insights about life. When we are facing north, our sensing tells us we are resting upon the earth—the physical below us. Our heads reach into the sky, intuiting what the senses cannot grasp—the non-physical above. Looking to the east where the sun rises, our feelings see promise in the day yet to come—emotions in our right brain. Turning to the west, our thinking goes over the events of the day—intellectual analysis in our left brain.

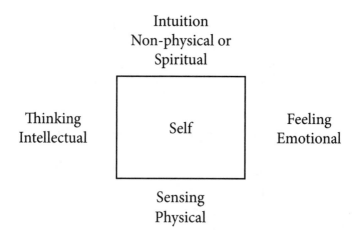

The top labels on each of the four sides of the diagram—sensing, feeling, thinking, intuition—are Jung's terms, and psychologists frequently use them to describe how people process information when communicating or solving problems. The bottom labels—physical, emotional, intellectual, spiritual— refer to a part of our self.

We can build a stronger sense of our self by understanding how these themes operate together in our personality. By developing them and bringing them into better balance, we can increase our effectiveness in all aspects of our life including planning our career.

These four sides automatically engage in varying degrees whenever we do anything. The more they engage in a balanced way, the more we are taking advantage of our potential. The more we have all four elements working in harmony, the more readily we present our true self to others and the more comfortable we feel in our activity. That is, honoring our physical, emotional, intellectual, non-physical or spiritual sides allows us to feel balanced overall and to lead a fulfilled, happy life.

Balance among the four does not mean giving equal weight to each in every instance. Any endeavor will require more or less of each of the four. Often, one aspect takes dominance, and the other three remain part of the picture but to a lesser degree. And, more important, our true nature will dictate that one play the larger role in most circumstances. So primarily, we want to identify what our true self looks like inside. How does each of us define balance? Does one aspect dominate our behavior? Which one? All the time? In which situations?

For instance, in relating to other people, our emphasis might be in doing activities together (physical), on feelings of rapport (emotional), on a meeting of the minds (intellectual), or on a commonality of purpose (non-physical or spiritual). In some of our relationships, these aspects may be more balanced than in others. In our daily work and in our career, we will have jobs that draw on these parts of us to varying degrees. We may be conscious of carrying out activities because they have to be done and we are able to do it (physical). We may have an affection for and interest in what we are doing (emotional). Our mind may be stimulated, and we may see enlightening relationships between ideas (intellectual). We may feel a sense of purpose in doing the work (spiritual).

We develop our sense of self through experiences right from the start and continue throughout our life. As babies, our bodies need to feel comfortable and secure. We connect to our surroundings through our senses of touch, sight, hearing, taste, and smell. Inborn predispositions to act in certain ways combine with environmental opportunities to create experiences in the areas of sensual awareness, observation, physical strength, and coordinated action. We feel physically comforted and secure. A sense of self with a goal of survival emerges. We reach out and engage people, seeking relationships and friendships. We want to feel cared for and to care for someone else. We are driven to be involved in successful relationships. The response we receive from our environment provides experiences in the emotional arena. We learn to express our feelings and to connect with the feelings of others. We act in ways that build our feeling of being comfortable. We are also driven towards thinking about ourselves in our environment, and we engage in experiences that use our logic for problem solving. We build knowledge and understanding that help us to survive, and we enhance our experiences using analysis, understanding, and planning. Our humanity seeks more, however. We sense that we are part of something bigger. We feel a connection to something that we cannot see and seek the wisdom that comes from contemplating what is outside of our self that we call non-physical, or spiritual.

Through all of our experiences, our self is connecting to the world. The nature of our connecting experience is unique to each of us, a combination of our genetic makeup and what our environment has called for and reinforced. One person's environment may have offered intense physical stimulation, relatively cold relationships, exposure to concrete ideas, and a concern with the practical realities of life. Another person may have had less physical stimulation, extremely warm emotional contact, discussions about abstract relationships, and an interest in more philosophical questions.

As a result of our unique experiences and predisposition, we each have developed the four sides—physical, emotional, intellectual, and spiritual—to varying degrees. They determine our self: every action we take, decision we make, thought we think draws upon them. Paying attention to the order in which they come into play helps us understand our self; the capacity which comes into play first has the biggest influence.

## PHYSICAL

The physical keeps all four aspects together, providing the foundation upon which the others develop—or not. Physical senses provide us with information about the physical world. Voice, expressions, and actions carry out intentions. A fully functioning body picks up and relays feelings and vibrations in a situation and, like a violin, magnifies them, creating a sharp awareness. The body, then, sets the stage for the other three aspects to manifest in a positive or negative way, depending upon the care that we give it. It allows powerful expression to thoughts and feelings, joyously when well cared for or angrily when not. A well-nourished physical body provides an environment conducive to the mental activity required for great thought; a deprived or abused one thinks irrationally or fearfully. And a relaxed and peaceful body generates heightened feelings for spiritual insight whereas one in turmoil has no chance to sense beyond the physical.

In the workplace, we are leading with our physical capacity and our senses when we carry out the following actions:

- Working energetically, with endurance, and/or with coordination
- Meeting deadlines
- Observing objects and monitoring activities
- Investigating thoroughly and in detail
- Doing what is practical and will work
- Following procedures with precision
- Organizing information systematically
- Following up on assigned tasks
- Adhering to standards
- Handling multiple tasks at once

To become more aware of your physical capacity, ask yourself:

- Do your physical mannerisms convey your meaning so that you effectively communicate, or do you give mixed messages. is your body language out of sync with your spoken words?
- Do you have high energy throughout the day, or does it significantly vary?
- When you are enthusiastic about something, do you feel it fully in your body, or do you remain unaware and separated from your feelings?

## *EMOTIONAL*

The emotional capacity determines the degree to which we feel a strong connection to the world and whether the bond is positive or negative, productive or non-productive. The emotional side and productive feelings bond us to another person and provide the energy to thoughts, providing impact for high interest projects. Physical performance improves under heightened emotions, and more innovative ideas emerge when engaged with the emotions.

Emotions are a communications pipeline between the situation and the self. They provide a rapid signal about whether a situation will help the self to survive or threaten its existence. Picture yourself in a situation with pipes containing a liquid connecting you and each person and key element in the situation. Pipes also connect everything else in the situation. The liquid in each pipe represents your emotions. It might be a peaceful blue or an intense red; warm, cool, boiling or icy; and flowing rapidly or slowly.

In the workplace, we are using our emotional capacity in a leading role when we carry out these actions:

- Coaching and interacting closely with others
- Negotiating that includes all participants
- Helping others learn and apply concepts
- Creating an environment in which others can excel
- Managing and utilizing strengths of others
- Anticipating needs of customers
- Bringing interpersonal issues out into the open
- Sensing hidden emotions
- Expressing care and emotional support
- Teaming and including others as appropriate

To become more aware of your emotional capacity, ask yourself these questions:

- Think about the situations in the past when you felt warm acceptance or empathy for others. Do you ever feel that now? Under what circumstances?
- Do you belong to a group in which positive emotions and support are shared?
- Are you working on a project now that draws on your high passion?

## INTELLECTUAL

Our intellectual capacity uses words and pictures to convey the reality of the world around us. We take them in through our senses and the mind organizes the information, storing it for later, drawing upon it to make relationships with other knowledge, and eventually creating new ideas to solve problems. Our intellectual side leads when we represent ideas with symbols and use logic to analyze something, identify cause and effect, or organize a knowledge base.

People assume that those with the greatest capacity for logic have the greatest minds. Analytical reasoning, they believe, enables us to arrive at the best solution to a problem, whether planning a winning business strategy, developing a theory to explain complex situations, or choosing a partner for life. Often, however, great minds stem not from using only the intellectual capacity but from continually developing each of the four capacities to a higher level and using them in an appropriate and balanced way.

In the workplace, our intellectual capacity is taking the lead role when we carry out these actions:

- Applying logic to structures and processes
- Identifying root causes of problems
- Deciding quickly on a best course
- Creating efficient systems
- Analyzing information for accuracy
- Synthesizing information

- Examining data for relevance and accuracy
- Questioning to bring out multiple views
- Judging efficiency of solutions
- Applying appropriate theories to situations

To become more aware of your intellectual capacity, consider the following:

- Think of an example in which you placed emphasis on your intellectual capacity. What aspects did you not consider? What happened as a result?

- We sometimes react without thinking things through adequately. Have you done this in a problem-solving situation? What results did you get? Could you have done differently—and gotten a better outcome?

- What sources of knowledge do you use to make decisions, and how current are they?

### Non-Physical or Spiritual

What explains the true story of a football team with the same players going from a two-win, ten-loss season one year to a ten-win, two-loss season the next? The players may have become stronger. They may have practiced the plays and their positions more. Or they may have learned new plays. But those factors alone could not create such an impact. A non-physical element had to contribute to the turnaround, such as a vision instilled by a new coach that brings out superior performance in each of the players. We cannot touch or feel or see or smell or hear a vision, but it exists and, as with a winning team, can have very real and physical effects. We describe such an element as non-physical or spiritual.

Our non-physical, or spiritual, side is all about believing and acting on what exists beyond the physical world at this time. It's about having a vision to bring something new into existence. It can result in a faith that will drive our actions towards an ideal situation or an envisioned goal. This gives us conviction and belief, strengths that we use to turn a vision into a reality. Our whole system flows with more power when we draw from our non-physical, or spiritual, conviction.

We know that each of us has this capacity because we see, for instance, how each of us has different levels of appreciation for artwork. One person will look at a painting and be transfixed because it speaks to something powerful within. Another will look at the same piece and see nothing worthy of a second glance, but they will be moved by a different one.

In the workplace, we are leading with our non-physical capacity when we carry out these actions:

- Brainstorming and generating alternatives
- Forecasting and predicting results
- Using imagination to visualize outcomes
- Talking about the big picture
- Monitoring knowledge and trends in one's industry
- Thinking out of the box
- Seeking ideas from a variety of perspectives
- Seeing possibilities in new ideas
- Intuiting the impact of decisions
- Seeing non-linear connections and integrating seemingly unrelated pieces
- Inventing a new product or service.
- Seeing a subtle trend that is key to a business strategy
- Anticipating a problem
- Persisting when everyone else is discouraged
- Using intuition to identify the reason for a success or failure

To become more aware of your non-physical or spiritual capacity, consider the following:

- Are you habitually more optimistic or pessimistic?

- When you face a challenge without the help of other people, do you stand alone or do you feel supported by a connection to something beyond the physical?

- Do you feel that there is a master plan for your life?

Our self becomes a stronger force within us when we develop our four capacities. But we need to keep them in balance. Otherwise one dominates and intimidates the others. In expressing a majestic idea, an orchestra conductor deploys the major sections—strings, woodwinds, brass, and percussion—according to a plan, using the right sections at the right time to achieve a desired effect. Similarly, our self orchestrates its physical, emotional, mental, and spiritual resources to bring about a certain result. And when these parts work together in harmony, we create glorious music, a majestic work of art.

When we are conscious of how these four parts are working within us, our self-awareness and self-understanding operate at their highest. We then know which parts are highly developed and tend to dominate, and which parts are less developed and require additional effort to deploy.

- Which of the four capacities do you think is strongest within you?

- Which has the least presence in your personality?

- If you were to be more creative in some way, what would you be doing more of?

## Career Dreams

There is more to our self than the part that solves problems and communicates with others. There is the part that dreams, sometimes with abandon. There is a chance that your past experiences may have dimmed those dreams. Are you looking forward to the future with the same anticipation and excitement as you did at times in the past? No? Do you think those dreams belong in the past because you can never make them real?

Think again. Dreams begin the journey along any path and give hint to what you will make real. Begin now to remember what you truly want. Place yourself in a comfortable position. Breathe deeply and relax all of your muscles. Linger over each of the following questions without rushing and let the answers, which you may have buried deeper and deeper over the succeeding years, rise up. Let them come naturally into your awareness from the same part of your mind that dreams.

What would make your life better now?

If you could change yourself in any way, what would you change?

If your body were different in any way, what would that be?

Think of the most satisfying relationship you have had in the past. What made it so good?

If you could use your thinking to solve any problem, what would that problem be?

What was a time when you felt connected to something bigger than yourself and everything was more meaningful?

What is your favorite song? Why do you like it so much?

Who is living a life you admire? What is that person doing that is worthwhile?

What in the world needs to be changed?

If you had economic and physical security, what would you do to have fun?

Think of a time in which you totally enjoyed what you were doing. What were you doing? What made it satisfying?

What was a favorite hobby in the past, and what did you enjoy about it?

What would a perfect day be like?

Picture in your mind an appealing place you have visited. What did you like about it?

What would your best friend suggest that you do?

What do you envision as the most ideal outcome at the end of your career path? What next step will help you get there?

## Accomplishments

We are looking for increased self-understanding to plan a future career that feeds our passions so that we are fulfilled and utilizes our strengths so that we are successful. Part of this heightened awareness comes from examining our past accomplishments. Under what circumstances did we succeed? What were we doing in them that was an expression of our creativity? What processes and knowledge did we use? What results were we creating and how did we feel about them?

The recognition that learning from past accomplishments is a key to future career success began with Bernard Haldane, PhD, in 1948 when he helped professionals to find career direction.[3] His innovative thinking differed from what most psychologists believed at the time— that certain personality characteristics determined success in specific jobs and, by identifying what traits a person had, they could determine where he or she would most likely succeed. John Crystal fully explicated the process of identifying past accomplishments in the early 1970s.[4] Arthur Miller used the process in his organizational programs. Richard Bolles included the full process in *What Color is Your Parachute?* In the 2010 version of that book, Bolles states that an understanding of abilities demonstrated in accomplishments is the most important part of a career counseling experience.[5] The process presented here builds upon this thinking and adds a technique from competency methodology, presented in Chapter 4, that systematically identifies unique interests and abilities that the individual has demonstrated in a number of settings.

Consider accomplishments from all areas of life. If we have been working for a while, we may think of successes only in past jobs and about career only in terms of job titles. A much stronger career identity emanates from past accomplishments in all areas of life, including paid jobs, volunteer projects, community activities, social activities, personal relationships, hobby activities, and leisure activities. Our achievements in these areas, especially the optional ones, those that we willingly gave time to, provide clues to our strengths and passions, and they will connect directly to an accurate career identify.

We develop through the experiences of every stage of our life, with those from a young age carrying significant influence. The manner in which we met our challenges at all ages contributes to our personality. They challenged our survival, and we responded with actions that brought success or failure, growth or retreat.

We all have a unique pattern of experiences. Have you ever seen two people who looked and acted exactly alike? Our brain, bodily features, organs, chemical makeup, and biological processes are different. A picture of a brain looks similar to other brains. But closer examination reveals the incredible uniqueness of each one. The folds are different, the neurons are clustered in different places, the gaps between the neurons are of different sizes, and the chemicals called neurotransmitters that move between the gaps are present in different amounts. We can say the same for every organ in our body and the communication channels between them.

We started life with a unique DNA sequence and since then have engaged in experiences that are unique to us. This combination has created a person who intensely enjoys and excels at some things, is good at many others, and performs adequately in a large number of activities.

We have a vast array of experiences, but only a few warrant highlighting as the foundation of our future career. These are your "key" experiences. When we look at our key experiences together, we will be able to see a theme as we look backward and a potential path as we look forward.

Bernard Haldane emphasized that in the experiences that are key for us:

- We took active part in making things happen.
- We enjoyed what we did.
- We had successes within the experience and, at least, a somewhat positive overall outcome.
- We felt proud of the result.

It takes effort to look back with an open mind. But we need to overcome the temptation to ignore the past. Only by looking back can we see that we have a potentially excellent career path comprised not of our job titles but of our experiences. The past will clue us in to our strengths and allow us to build an appealing résumé, talk about ourselves positively in networking meetings, and have examples at hand that will enable us to win in interviews.

When we look back, we might first recall the negative experiences, or if they strongly impacted us, we might do just the opposite and completely block them from our memory. In either case, we can't ignore them. We must first acknowledge them. Then we must get past them so we can see all of our history and learn from the good and the so-called bad. Finally, we must recognize which experiences stand out and contribute positively to our productive career identity.

In looking back, we also need to overcome the habit of comparing ourselves to others. We tend to shy away from fully embracing an accomplishment if we know another person performed more effectively in the same or a similar situation. This kind of comparing always results in our feeling second best and does not serve us here. Only we—not outsiders— can judge the importance of the experience and the quality of the results.

Some people mistakenly count as accomplishments only those activities that have received a reward or recognition by others. Do not limit your search in that way.

Review all of your past jobs, social interactions, hobbies, and community activities for positive feelings about what you did (the actions you took) and the results you achieved. You will likely more easily identify activities with external, or physical, action, as in playing sports or preparing a report. Others that you might gloss over, thinking they do not matter, come from internal activity, such as "Inspiration in a beautiful place." In this case, your presence in a particular place might have brought about profound appreciation for the natural world and made you feel connected to creative forces. These experiences are equally important.

Use the following list as a guide in examining your past for accomplishments you deem important. Write the title of one or more accomplishments you are able to remember now next to each description.

Write those that don't fit in a category on the lines below. Don't worry if nothing much comes to mind during this initial look back.

- Successful project in a recent job
- Creative idea about how to position a service or product
- Productive team experience
- Recognition for your expertise
- Using your knowledge
- Being creative
- Making a speech
- Holding a meeting
- Contributing to brainstorming
- Forming relationships and networking successfully
- Social activity
- Inspiration in a beautiful place
- Adventure
- Improving a process
- Improving quality
- Successful sport
- Helping a team to win
- Family activity
- Customer relationship
- Organizing an event
- Planning a project
- _____
- _____
- _____

## *PEAK EXPERIENCES*

We will feel our uniqueness most fully when we are invoking our strongest talents and fulfilling many of our values. Abraham Maslow coined the phrase "peak experiences" to describe a person's most satisfying and memorable experiences. At those times, the person has fully expressed his or her true self and is actualized. The result is a feeling of significance, unity with the world, personal power, and efficacy. A feeling of ecstasy makes time stand still.

Everyone has had peak experiences in the past and will have more in the future. When you see and relive a peak experience from the past, you get a feeling of what your whole career can be like. Past peak experiences answer key career questions: What is most important to you? What enlivens you and brings a sense of supernatural fulfillment? What do you do most effectively?

Some of your peak experiences may elude you; you may even think you have had none. Not true! Your growth towards a healthy career will cause them to rise cautiously to the surface of your memory where you can examine them and learn from them and then allow more to come to your attention.

As a career counselor, I have led people to discover their peak experiences in both individual and group sessions. Everyone has had some kind of peak experience around age eleven or in the fifth grade. At this age, you have developed individual interests, and you are old enough to go off on your own walking, taking a bus, skateboarding, or riding a bike. And, importantly, you are not yet struggling to find your identity group. Here are some that clients have discovered from around this age:

- Organizing creative activities as a baby sitter
- Hiking in the woods and feeling a part of nature
- Planning a party with friends
- Skateboarding with a newly learned style
- Reading and being engrossed in a story
- Sharing in a friendship

- Watching a sunrise
- Playing video games
- Winning in a sports competition
- Being in a band
- Dancing in a ballet
- Listening to music
- Riding a horse
- Fixing a bike

Identify your own peak experiences and write them here:

_____

_____

_____

_____

In this section we have implemented a method of identifying accomplishments that can help us to learn what we need to know about ourselves to be a more effective career planner.

- When you looked back in this chapter, do you have a easy or hard time seeing accomplishments?

- If you could be involved in any kind of new experience, what would it be? Where might you have done something similar in the past?

- Was it more enlightening to see a time when you were rewarded by someone else or when you were your own judge of the value of the experience?

# EXPANDING EXPERIENCES

Awareness of your important accomplishments establishes the foundation for finding work that fulfills you. Now you need to build upon this base, using the actions implemented in the accomplishments to understand your strengths and all of the work possibilities open to you. You will also expand your accomplishments into compelling and credible stories that will build your confidence and improve your résumé, networking skills, and interviewing success.

Your career up until now is like a movie that stars your self as the main character. To understand this character, you need to package and frame the actions to see how you responded to specific challenges. From seeing a specific scene, you can make an inference about the capabilities and interests of the main character that set the stage for your subsequent scenes and whole life. Focusing on that frame, you can expand key experiences from your past jobs and other parts of your life such as hobbies, social activities, or volunteer activities.

Expanding your accomplishment experiences will be done following the steps of STARS. The acronym, STAR, was first used by industrial psychologists in the mid 1950s to carry out a job analysis through behavioral event interviews. I began using it in career counseling sessions in the early 1980s. It, or one with a similar acronym, is now used extensively as a part of virtually all career counseling experiences. The last S is added here because it's important and helpful to review the actions alone and with others to identify strength themes.

Here are the steps involved. First, summarize the whole experience in a title. Then follow STARS:

S – Situation: Write the key elements of the situation.

T – Task: Identify the specific challenge you saw or your goal (this understanding might come after you have completed the sheet, and so it is okay to leave it until the end).

A – Actions: Write four or more action phrases about what you did in response to the challenge you saw.

R – Results: Show a quantitative or qualitative statement on the results.

S – Strengths: List some of the strength themes that can be seen.

Page 28 shows an example of how a career searcher, Ryan, completed a worksheet to learn more about his talents and strengths.

Beginning on page 29, you have seven STARS Story worksheets, each devoted to filling out information about a different experience. These forms use the five steps of STARS to help reveal insights about those experiences.

The experience you choose for each worksheet can be of any time duration. It can be a five-minute negotiation or a two-year management of a relationship with a key customer. It can be a short, intimate discussion with a friend or the whole friendship. It can be a specific sports contest or an engagement with a sports activity over years. The STARS will package it. The key is to be specific. Career counselors agree that expanding seven experiences yields a useful picture, so fill out all seven pages.

Use the questions of the worksheet as a guide. Most important, keep asking, "What did I do to do that?" or, "What did that look like?" Your answers will bring out the talents and knowledge you were using to create a result that you valued.

Recalling the actions you took will enrich the meaning of the experience for you and enhance its impact as you talk about it. Put yourself in the situation and remember actions that were external and you could see. Then remember actions that were internal and that you could not see, such as identifying the knowledge you were using or the thought process you went through. If your accomplishment is watching a movie that was meaningful to you, your actions might have included responding spontaneously to humor, critiquing the acting methods, putting the theme into historical perspective, feeling a sense of activism, or feeling the emotions of the characters.

Most likely, you will not think of all of the important actions on your own. Your relatively limited perspective will allow you to identify only some of your abilities and knowledge. Some of your feelings and assumptions will prevent you from seeing everything that you were doing. A person who does not see him- or herself as a leader, for instance, will not notice actual instances of leadership. You might also take for granted some of your best abilities and not notice them. If you could ask a fish about its abilities, it might not include swimming as one of them because that ability is so much a part of what it is. Therefore, it is essential that you go over your experiences with another person.

Subsequent to his work with transitioning professionals through a successful business, Dr. Bernard Haldane developed The Dependable Strengths Articulation Process, which is a group process presented by schools and agencies to help people move ahead in their careers. It emphasizes identifying stories of good experiences, telling them to others in a small group setting, and getting feedback from group members about the skills they were using. Group members also suggest improvements for talking about strengths as well as occupational possibilities and how to pursue them. The process is laid out in detail by Professor Jerald Forster, Ph.D. in *Articulating Strengths Together*.[6]

In his workshops, Richard Bolles coined and popularized the term "trioing" to describe one of the ways of doing this. One person relates his or her story. Another asks questions that bring out additional actions. A third records abilities and knowledge used. Both provide feedback about what they hear. Having two assistants in this process will help you see more interests and abilities than you knew you had, see your best talents, and boost your confidence.

If two other people for a trioing activity are not available, one other person—a friend or a co-worker—will work very well. Take these steps with a partner:

1. Read your experience from the STARS worksheet to your partner.

2. Your partner should write notes on the strengths he or she hears.

3. Your partner asks questions to bring out more of the experience.

4. You talk about the strengths you see.

5. Your partner adds other strengths he or she noted.

6. You add new discoveries from the discussion to your STARS worksheet in the Strengths section.

An experienced counselor can provide insight that will greatly increase the effectiveness of using past accomplishments to understand strengths. Everyone has blind spots that prevent recognizing past accomplishments and themes, and a counselor will recognize this and tactfully lead you back so that you gain an objective and strong appreciation of yourself.

### New Insights about Strengths

*Julie was working as a clinical trials manager in which her analytic and leadership skills were important. When she sought career counseling because she was not happy with her job she had no idea of what she might enjoy doing. As her career counselor, I got her talking about her past. With probing through experiences she was happy to forget, she recalled an accomplishment in which she won a race. Listening and asking insightful questions led her to surface building doll houses. The permission that counseling provided to be who she really was resulted in her recalling her meticulously attending to the varnishing and paint she used over the card board. The recognition that this was a physical kind of strength brought back other physical memories, such as dirt biking with her dad and brothers. Thanks to this appreciation, she is pursuing a career in design.*

## Sample STARS Story

Title:_____Teaching Web Navigation_____

**S** (Situation) – What were key elements of the situation and what was your role?

   *-Teaching web design to adult students.*

   *-Topic was web navigation.*

**T** (Task) – What was your task, challenge, or goal?

   *- Put them at ease and keep them interested.*

   *- Relate to their experience.*

**A** (Actions) – What actions did you take, what did they look like, and what did you do to carry them out? How did you respond to challenges? What else did you do?

   *- Introduced topic in conversational way.*

   *- Had calm and relaxed manner.*

   *- Asked them to remember times they needed to find their way.*

   *- Used humor.*

   *- Organized small groups to brainstorm.*

   *- Had students cut out colored shapes.*

**R** (Results) – What was the result or what changed in your view?

   *- Students said they enjoyed it.*

   *- All completed the assignment.*

**S** (Strengths) – What characteristics do you see in yourself? (Have partner question and suggest additions.)

   *Sense of humor, emotionally aware, sensitive to information overload, savvy about learning differences, proceed in slow and orderly way, imaginative, compassionate, artistic, hands-on teaching style, learner-centered.*

## STARS Story #1

*Title:* _____

**S** *(Situation) – What were key elements of the situation and what was your role?*

- _____

- _____

**T** *(Task) – What was your task, challenge, or goal?*

- _____

- _____

**A** *(Actions) – What actions did you take, what did they look like, and what did you do to carry them out? How did you respond to challenges? What else did you do?*

- _____

- _____

- _____

- _____

**R** *(Results) – What was the result or what changed in your view?*

- _____

- _____

**S** *(Strengths) –What characteristics do you see in yourself? (Have partner question and suggest additions.)*

- _____

- _____

- _____

- _____

## STARS Story #2

*Title:* _____

**S** *(Situation) – What were key elements of the situation and what was your role?*

- _____

- _____

**T** *(Task) – What was your task, challenge, or goal?*

- _____

- _____

**A** *(Actions) – What actions did you take, what did they look like, and what did you do to carry them out? How did you respond to challenges? What else did you do?*

- _____

- _____

- _____

- _____

**R** *(Results) – What was the result or what changed in your view?*

- _____

- _____

**S** *(Strengths) –What characteristics do you see in yourself? (Have partner question and suggest additions.)*

- _____

- _____

- _____

- _____

## STARS Story #3

Title: _____

**S** *(Situation) – What were key elements of the situation and what was your role?*

- _____

- _____

**T** *(Task) – What was your task, challenge, or goal?*

- _____

- _____

**A** *(Actions) – What actions did you take, what did they look like, and what did you do to carry them out? How did you respond to challenges? What else did you do?*

- _____

- _____

- _____

- _____

**R** *(Results) – What was the result or what changed in your view?*

- _____

- _____

**S** *(Strengths) –What characteristics do you see in yourself? (Have partner question and suggest additions.)*

- _____

- _____

- _____

- _____

## STARS Story #4

*Title:* _____

**S** *(Situation) – What were key elements of the situation and what was your role?*

- _____
- _____

**T** *(Task) – What was your task, challenge, or goal?*

- _____
- _____

**A** *(Actions) – What actions did you take, what did they look like, and what did you do to carry them out? How did you respond to challenges? What else did you do?*

- _____
- _____
- _____
- _____

**R** *(Results) – What was the result or what changed in your view?*

- _____
- _____

**S** *(Strengths) –What characteristics do you see in yourself? (Have partner question and suggest additions.)*

- _____
- _____
- _____
- _____

## STARS Story #5

*Title:* _____

*S (Situation) – What were key elements of the situation and what was your role?*

- _____
- _____

*T (Task) – What was your task, challenge, or goal?*

- _____
- _____

*A (Actions) – What actions did you take, what did they look like, and what did you do to carry them out? How did you respond to challenges? What else did you do?*

- _____
- _____
- _____
- _____

*R (Results) – What was the result or what changed in your view?*

- _____
- _____

*S (Strengths) –What characteristics do you see in yourself? (Have partner question and suggest additions.)*

- _____
- _____
- _____
- _____

## STARS Story #6

*Title:* _____

**S** *(Situation) – What were key elements of the situation and what was your role?*

- _____
- _____

**T** *(Task) – What was your task, challenge, or goal?*

- _____
- _____

**A** *(Actions) – What actions did you take, what did they look like, and what did you do to carry them out? How did you respond to challenges? What else did you do?*

- _____
- _____
- _____
- _____

**R** *(Results) – What was the result or what changed in your view?*

- _____
- _____

**S** *(Strengths) –What characteristics do you see in yourself? (Have partner question and suggest additions.)*

- _____
- _____
- _____
- _____

**STARS Story #7**

*Title:* _____

*S (Situation) – What were key elements of the situation and what was your role?*

- _____
- _____

*T (Task) – What was your task, challenge, or goal?*

- _____
- _____

*A (Actions) – What actions did you take, what did they look like, and what did you do to carry them out? How did you respond to challenges? What else did you do?*

- _____
- _____
- _____
- _____

*R (Results) – What was the result or what changed in your view?*

- _____
- _____

*S (Strengths) –What characteristics do you see in yourself? (Have partner question and suggest additions.)*

- _____
- _____
- _____
- _____

In this section you learned how to identify the actions, interests, and abilities that you demonstrated in your past accomplishments. These actions will be a part of your future career success.

- Did you identify some actions, interests, and abilities that were new to you?

- What impact did working with a partner have in increasing your self-understanding? What abilities and actions did you miss that your partner helped you uncover?

- Which strength are you most interested in using in the future? In what possible occupational role(s) you can use it?

In the next chapter, you will use the actions you uncovered to help identify the preferred characteristics of your career.

## CHAPTER THREE

# CAREER CHOICE POINTS

In expanding our experiences into STARS stories, we listed a number of actions, both those which could be observed from outside of us and those that took place on the inside, such as what we were feeling, our thought processes, and the knowledge we were using. All of those actions happened because certain parts of us became engaged. All were an expression of who we are.

The following diagram lists six personal considerations that lie behind our career. Those that are closest to our personality are listed on the left side. They are the result of a combination of our inherited DNA and our early nurturing. The first, our **Values and Needs**, most closely reflects our true inner self. Every action we take creates a result. Some of the results satisfy a deeply held ideal; others satisfy a need. Our values and needs come closest to defining who we really are. We are using them as a choice point in our career when we make a courageous decision based on what is most important to us. People who leave a job with steady pay to pursue a dream are acting on their values and needs.

We consider the second choice point, our **Intelligences**, when we embark on an education and development path. Our intelligences refer to our potential to learn the processes and knowledge of an occupation. They derive from both our given genetic makeup as well as learning techniques we have acquired through schooling and practice. This choice point becomes important when we select a field of study because we naturally learn and retain its processes and knowledge and so are able to achieve our highest possible level of performance in it.

It would seem that choosing a career we value and for which we have the required intelligences would insure career success. But more is involved. In specific situations, we don't always follow our values and intelligences. Often we follow our habits of responding in those kinds of situations. Everyone displays a pattern of actions that have become habitual, called **Preferences**, the third choice point. They describe actions we take spontaneously and naturally in response to a challenge. We become known for these actions which make up our personality type. We invoke this choice point when we choose work projects or other activities because they require parts of us that we prefer to use. People who understand the power of this dynamic know also what they prefer to avoid, their blind spots, and team with people who bring different preferences and other perspectives.

Next in the diagram is the fourth choice point, our **Interests**, those actions that draw on our greatest enthusiasms. We can choose to engage in activities that we find fun, and when we are having fun, we perform at a higher level, are more happy, and are more healthy. We can also determine that we don't feel our interests strongly enough and decide to increase our self-knowledge by engaging in a variety of new activities and seeing which ones we like to do.

The fifth choice point in the diagram is our **Environmental Support Desires**. We can choose a work setting in which we are happy and feel supported. We can identify company and management policies that bring out our best and find matching organizations.

The sixth choice point is our **Abilities and Knowledge**. Everything we do requires some level of expertise, from next to none for mundane tasks done by rote to others demanding refined skills and years of education, as in open-heart surgery. We invoke this choice point when we choose a work situation that uses the abilities, skills, and knowledge we have developed on past jobs or in educational endeavors.

Early in the science of choosing a career the emphasis was on "traits." But people discovered that traits have a unique meaning for each person. Then the word "temperaments" was used, because people are made up of a mixture that influences the impact of each element, just like in the tempering of steel. Here we are using the term "choice points" because our career is a process in which we can make a choice to increase our self understanding to create an ideal career path that will result in meaning and success. When we choose our highest priority at each choice point, we are operating in our area of priority competence. When we make other choices at each point, we might be risking to discover new things about ourselves and preparing to build new capacities for unknown excitement in the future. Or, we might be making the choice to be complacent.

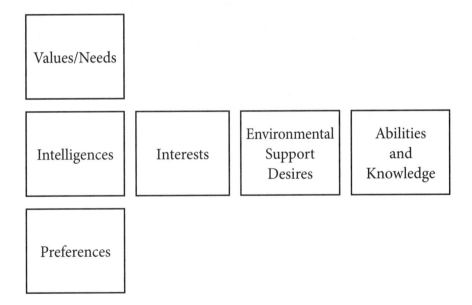

## Values and Needs

We can all appreciate the benefits that work brings to us. They range from the physical, such as financial reward that provides physical comfort and safety, to the non-physical or spiritual, such as the joy from obtaining knowledge, making a discovery, or having a spiritual insight. Abraham Maslow emphasized that we seek to satisfy first the most crucial needs, those we need for bare subsistence (food, water, shelter, etc.). Only once we have met those do we move to satisfy another level of needs. The hierarchy of needs moves from the very physical to the more spiritual, each level replacing the previous one as the impetus for our actions. Not everyone advances along all levels.

Maslow's hierarchy of needs from highest to lowest is:

- Aesthetic
- Understanding
- Knowledge
- Self-actualizing
- Esteem or Ego
- Love & Belonging
- Safety & Security
- Physiological

Maslow's list verbalizes what we have known for thousands of years about the most basic and important ways that people differ from one another.[1] Physical needs are at the bottom and include insuring the health of our body, fixing that leak, and making processes such as production lines work in the world. The focus is on the individual. Many people find complete satisfaction at this level; they seek for no more. They derive meaning from what they can see. At the opposite end of the list, at the top, the non-physical needs include inventing, negotiating peace between warring parties, and creating designs. People at this level seek to make a significant contribution to the world at large, well beyond a person's immediate family or community. The middle holds the emotional needs, which go beyond the individual focus of the lower level but not as far as that of the highest levels. Here the person reaches out to other people, teaching, caring for others, and feeling a strong sense of self. Also in the middle are the intellectual needs, which include researching to acquire new knowledge, understanding, and planning.

We can place our values and needs that stand behind career decisions on this hierarchy. These include seeing the results of work, achieving a certain level of status, working for a successful company, adding to beauty, having time for family, independence, using abilities, competing, practicing altruism, contributing to knowledge, advocating for a cause, being spiritual, and inventing something.

We see the hierarchy at work within us every day. If we worry about our job security, we cannot concentrate well enough to read a poem. If we have a tight deadline for a project, our mind will not leave it to enjoy a movie. We look first to filling our own needs, but we reach a higher level of performance when we also understand and fill the needs of others. Increasing our understanding to include those outside of us injects more passion into our work, and we perform more effectively in our career activities. When we knowingly aim to satisfy needs that both we and others identify as important, we feel doubly charged to do great work.

### *Discovering Values*

*Susan landed her first job after majoring in business in product management with a consumer products company. After success there, she moved to sales where she also succeeded. After a number of promotions, her performance started to level off, and at mid-age, she was laid off. In her younger years, her need for financial security fueled her extensive efforts to excel, and she enjoyed the resulting monetary rewards and promotions. However, she never really made her own decision about what she wanted for her life and career. Now, without a job and with plenty of free time, she decided to discover her real preferences, intelligences, interests, and abilities. A volunteer position with Special Olympics caught her eye, and through the job, she learned that working in social services now gave her much more meaning. She found helping to improve the lives of other people motivated her and rewarded her efforts. Eventually, she found a position in program development for a social agency.*

People often value different kinds of results, depending on the life role they are filling. We all play roles as students, wage earners, partners, family members, citizens, friends, and hobbyists, most at the same time and each with its own value. Sometimes the differences in needs for the different roles can be striking. As a wage earner, Franz Kafka worked quite happily as an insurance executive. As a second, possibly more crucial part of his career, he wrote existential novels such as *Metamorphosis*. Some people who are extremely competitive at work show the opposite characteristic when they are with friends on the weekend.

Working in a job you value because of the results you create may not be possible early in your career. You may first have to get involved in an occupation that allows you to use your abilities, skills, and knowledge in an industry in high demand before transferring them to the field you desire. Many industries require the same occupational skills and knowledge making transitioning to a different industry easier than one might think. Managerial, business processes, and customer services jobs, for example, exist in every industry. After gaining experience and building a reputation in one industry, you may move to another that encompasses the results you value most.

Have you ever had a situation that unequivocally defined your values? Our country had such an instance when it passed the Civil Rights Bill. That action clearly communicated that individual freedom was our highest value. A presidency has a defining moment. Many people think that calling for landing a man on the moon was the defining moment of the Kennedy presidency. You may have had experiences that brought out your values. When have you felt strong satisfaction in seeing the results of your work? Have you expressed an opinion in a political discussion? What is something that made you angry? Imagining a perfect career future, if you could make a change in the world, what would it be?

You may not be able to think of a defining moment now, but you have lots of evidence about what your values are. In writing your STARS stories, you carried out a large number of actions. Those actions were an indication of your values. Referring back to those stories, use the following chart to categorize many of the actions you have identified into the eight groupings identified by Maslow. The box with the most actions is probably one of your primary values.

### Actions and Values

Look at the actions in your STARS stories. Identify those that express the needs and values listed below and place them in the appropriate section of this chart.

| Self-actualizing<br>Ex: Seeking the challenge of an adventure | Knowledge<br>Ex: Researching past practices | Understanding<br>Ex: Seeing relationships in data | Aesthetic<br>Ex: Contributing a new insight |
|---|---|---|---|
| Physiological<br>Ex: Making sure things function | Safety & Security<br>Ex: Saving resources | Love & Belonging<br>Ex: Intimate discussion | Esteem or Ego<br>Ex: Stubbornly standing firm. |

# INTELLIGENCES

We need to know what we can do naturally and what we can learn in order to perform at our best. Historically, the word "aptitude" referred to the potential to develop one's given abilities. But we limited those abilities, and our definition of aptitude, to what we could measure with an objectively validated test—those dealing with reasoning, spatial relations, clerical skills, and physical skills. We now acknowledge that people differ in their aptitudes, in how they learn; using one instructional method to teach everyone in a classroom will not bring success to all. Howard Gardner introduced the word "intelligences" to describe these differences.[2] Through observational research, he identified eight ways that people learn. We see these categories as both the means by which we acquire knowledge and the capabilities of our mind. These broad intelligence categories are:

- Intrapersonal
- Logical-Mathematical
- Verbal-Linguistic
- Interpersonal
- Visual-Spatial
- Naturalist
- Musical-Rhythmic
- Bodily-Kinesthetic

An article at the New Horizons for Learning Web site describes each intelligence in this way:

Intrapersonal intelligence involves understanding one's inner world of emotions and thoughts, and growing in the ability to control them and work with them consciously. It may be exercised through participating in independent projects, reading illuminating books, journal-writing, imaginative activities and games, and finding quiet places for reflection.

Logical-Mathematical intelligence involves number and computing skills, recognizing patterns and relationships, timeliness and order, and the ability to solve different kinds of problems through logic. It may be exercised through classifying and sequencing activities, playing number and logic games, and solving various kinds of puzzles.

Verbal-Linguistic intelligence involves reading, writing, speaking, and conversing in one's own or foreign languages. It may be exercised through reading interesting books, playing word board or card games, listening to recordings, using various kinds of computer technology, and participating in conversation and discussions.

Interpersonal involves understanding how to communicate with and understand other people and how to work collaboratively. It may be exercised through cooperative games, group projects and discussions, multicultural books and materials, and dramatic activities or role-playing.

Visual-Spatial intelligence involves visual perception of the environment, the ability to create and manipulate mental images, and the orientation of the body in space. It may be developed through experiences in the graphic and plastic arts, sharpening observation skills, solving mazes and other spatial tasks, and exercises in imagery and active imagination.

Naturalist intelligence involves understanding the natural world of plants and animals, noticing their characteristics, and categorizing them; it generally involves keen observation and the ability to classify other things as well. It may be exercised by exploring nature, making collections of objects, studying them, and grouping them.

Musical-Rhythmic intelligence involves understanding and expressing oneself through music and rhythmic movements or dance, or composing, playing, or conducting music. It may be exercised by listening to a variety of recordings, engaging in rhythmic games and activities, and singing, dancing, or playing various instruments.

Bodily-Kinesthetic intelligence involves physical coordination and dexterity, using fine and gross motor skills, and expressing oneself or learning through physical activities. It may be exercised by playing with blocks and other construction materials, dancing, playing various active sports and games, participating in plays or make-believe, and using various kinds of manipulatives to solve problems or to learn.[3]

A person high in a specific intelligence will be able to learn easily in it, retain information pertinent to it, and develop related skills and abilities to a high level. This will enable him or her to act in a variety of situations with expertise.

It is important, however, not to let intelligences play too big of a role in determining career direction. Some people, for instance, shy away from entering an occupation with a reputation for people with a high intelligence out of fear of not being able to compete. Most people are average in many of the intelligences and, with interest and hard work in a valued area, are able to make significant contributions. Too often people turn from an interest because they fear they lack adequate intelligence in the area. It would be better to pursue their interest with the optimism that they will be able to find a role that fits their intelligences.

### Intelligent Career Decision

*Jill always felt most capable in interpersonal interactions. Her easy-going manner put others at ease, and her listening skills allowed them to open up to her and feel even more comfortable. Showing empathy in her discussions, she readily helped them understand how to take action to solve their own problems. But when a job opened in the research department in her company, she considered applying for it. She performed well in research and thought the work made significant contributions to society, but she knew that she would not achieve her highest level of excellence in it. As much as she enjoyed the work, she knew her greatest expertise lay elsewhere. Instead of applying to that job, Jill opted to wait for a position in which she could use her skills in directly influencing people. She later found a position that used her skills and matched her interests, one that enabled her to be a clinician as well as a researcher.*

As employees, we must continually learn in order to keep up with the demands for knowledge and expertise in our job. As career and job searchers, we can recognize what our strongest intelligences are and engage in learning activities that take advantage of them. But we need not limit ourselves only to our best mode of learning; we can also develop our other intelligences so that we can learn in new ways. This will increase our efficiency in learning, improve many of our problem-solving activities, and open some doors to new knowledge.

A survey to assess the strength of each of your intelligences is at: http://literacyworks.org/mi/assessment/findyourstrengths.html

To further understand your intelligences, ask yourself these questions:

- What classes in school were relatively easy for you? Those using your body such as physical education or auto shop? Those that required reflection such as literature? Those that required skills with people, such as communications? Those that used your visual perception, such as photography? Those that brought out your rhythm, such as music? Those that involved verbalizing and talking about ideas such as history? Those that enabled you to use your logical brain to analyze such as math? Those that drew on an instinctual understanding of natural processes such as botany?

- What kind of information do you remember easily?

- When you have a fear of learning, what is the subject? Which intelligence does it draw upon?

## Actions and Intelligences

The actions in our STARS stories give clues as to how we learn. To help you to see your intelligence themes, write the Actions from your stories under the intelligence that was most responsible for each one's success.

| Interpersonal<br><br>Example: Making friends | Verbal-Linguistic<br><br>Ex: Writing a poem | Logical-Mathematical<br><br>Ex: Solving a research problem | Intrapersonal<br><br>Ex: Appealing to the soul in people |
|---|---|---|---|
| Bodily-Kinesthetic<br><br>Ex: athletic coordination | Visual-Spatial<br><br>Ex: Drawing in three dimensions | Naturalist<br><br>Ex: Getting a garden to grow | Musical-Rhythmic<br><br>Ex: Playing an instrument by ear |

# PREFERENCES

As a result of our genetic predisposition and our early experiences, we use and energize some of our capacities more than others.[4] Over the years, thanks to constant practice, these have developed into actions we perform naturally, usually competently, and often without thinking. They become our preferences, our personality habits that cause us to react to a challenge in a certain way.

The next time you are in a business meeting, notice that you can probably predict the kind of comments certain people will make. Some always summarize, others provide a practical example, and another identifies how people will be impacted. Each individual has built a unique habit of responding to his or her environment—processing information in a certain way, noticing some things and not others, and acting upon his or her analysis of the situation. Our preference for how to react to a situation depends upon three categories: direction, or where we handle the situation, inside us or outside; content, or what we perceive about the situation; and process, or what we do with the information we get.

The first category is the **direction we are facing**. If we are reflecting, experiencing, assessing, or understanding, we are facing inward, and the activity is in our inner world. Jung called this introversion. If we are acting, expressing ideas, or creating an impact, we are facing outward, and the activity occurs in the outer world. He called this extraversion. We need to use both to solve problems—acquiring information and processing it in our minds and then testing theories or ideas in the physical world or against others' ideas—but we learn to prefer one over the other. A person who prefers introversion will be effective, comfortable, and stress free in a job that requires more listening than presenting, such as in project management. A person who prefers extraversion will do well in a role that requires quick acting and little thinking about theory in isolation, as in teaching first graders. Jung called this preference an attitude because we are conscious of both and are able to move from one to other, just like an airplane adjusts its attitude when it moves from taking off to cruising.

The second category is **content**. Every action involves a subject matter, either physical or non-physical, that we perceive. Our five senses perceive physical information, providing us with a rich awareness of the look, touch, feel, sound, and smell of the world about us. Jung called this sensing. We also have an ability to perceive non-physical information, which Jung called intuition.

A person who prefers sensing may excel in a position that requires being very observant of facts, such as an auditor. A person high in intuition fits into a position that requires a lot of strategic thinking, such as a marketing executive. Jung called this a function because it explains the kind of thing we do, how we function. We will be more conscious and aware of one content function. The other will be more in our unconscious, according to Jung.

The third category is **process**. Every action also results from the way we process the information we perceive. When we attach a value to it and emotionally detect its quality, we are using what Jung referred to as feeling. We can also mentally process information by logically and sequentially seeing cause-and-effect relationships. Jung called this thinking. People high in feeling have a good fit in their jobs when, for instance, they must form close relationships based on empathy, as in counseling. Those high in thinking do well in jobs that require them to think deeply to see logical relationships, as in computer programming. This is also a function, with one side being primarily in our conscious awareness, and the other being primarily in our unconscious.

### Flexibility in Conveying Capacities through Language

*Caroline's résumé contained all of the experiences needed to highlight her deep interpersonal skills for a residency position that coached student clinicians. But the wording of her résumé gave the impression that her strengths lay more in the intellectual arena and that she might be impersonal in her interactions with students. Her natural attention towards thinking and her habitual preferences towards logic came out in the action phrases she used to describe her past work as a teacher in an inner city junior high school. To get an interview for the residency position, she needed to understand her natural preferences and how they affected the language she used and then to extend her view of her capacities so that she included more feeling language in her résumé. Beyond this one application, Caroline saw how she would benefit from being clear to her self about the kind of person she was and the kind of residency she should pursue.*

A very effective personality inventory that will give you a reliable, objective view of your personality according to Jung's view of tendencies and attention designed by David Keirsey can be taken here: www. advisorteam.com/temperament_sorter/register.asp?partid=1

Donna Dunning, in *What's Your Type of Career*, presents the strengths and workplace implications of all of the types identified by Jung and explained further in the Myers Briggs Type Indicator and in Keirsey's work.[4] She presents the following information for the eight types created by combining each attitude with each function.

- Introverted Sensing: specializing, stabilizing, organizing details, following procedures.
- Extraverted Sensing: acting, adapting, living in the moment, entertaining, being practical.
- Introverted Feeling: caring, connecting, appreciating, nurturing, working in harmony.
- Extraverted Feeling: contributing, cooperating, developing rapport, expressing.
- Introverted Thinking: examining, evaluating, analyzing logically, being competent.
- Extraverted Thinking: expediting, directing, deciding, structuring, getting results.
- Introverted Intuition: interpreting, implementing, creating and organizing ideas, applying.

Extraverted Intuition: exploring, innovating, initiating, inspiring, handling change.

To better understand your preferences, look at one of your accomplishments, and ask, "What personality preferences accounted for the success?" Look at a failure and ask, "What accounted for the failure?" Look at one of your hobbies. Is a personality preference a reason why you like it?

### Actions and Preferences

Look at your STARS stories again and the actions you were taking. Consider each action in relation to the pairs of aspects for the three categories: direction—introversion and extraversion, content—sensing and intuition, and process—feeling and thinking. Place the actions you listed in your STARS in the column under the most relevant category.

| Introvert Sensing<br>Ex: Observing detail | Introvert Feeling<br>Ex: Empathizing | Introvert Thinking<br>Ex: Logical analysis | Introvert Intuition<br>Ex: Seeing big picture |
|---|---|---|---|
| Extravert Sensing<br>Ex: Acting properly and quickly | Extravert Feeling<br>Ex: Expressing emotion such as care | Extravert Thinking<br>Ex: Directing others activities | Extravert Intuition<br>Ex: Planning with foresight |

# INTERESTS

We naturally gravitate to activities that feed our interests. And when our jobs hold those interests, we want to go to work, sometimes regardless of the results we create, because we enjoy the activities for their own sake. An artist enjoys painting regardless of whether a person buys the artwork. A musician enjoys playing regardless of whether anyone is listening. Writers write, leaders lead, researchers research, helpers help, organizers organize, all for the pure pleasure of working in what they enjoy. We feel a sense of satisfaction with nearly every action we take when it connects to our interests. Our work continually feeds us. We think about it with joy. We work harder. We exert a positive influence on our co-workers. And time passes by without our noticing because the activity totally consumes us.

Career researcher John Holland identified six interest themes to describe people and jobs.[4] The theme names follow, with one example of an activity that fits the theme.

- Realistic: carrying out physical activities
- Investigative: researching information
- Artistic: seeing things from a new perspective
- Social: helping people
- Enterprising: influencing and leading people
- Conventional: overseeing procedures and operations.

Identifying the theme that captures our primary interests helps us to find occupations we like. If we choose to work in a job that matches our highest themes, we have a high probability of enjoying the work as long as we have adequate ability in it. On the flip side, Holland also showed how the themes can help us understand conflicts between ourselves and our jobs. For example, we may see that our highest interest theme is opposite that of a job we are in.[5]

A reasonably priced online test to help you identify your interests is available at www.careerkey.org.

## Importance of Interests

*When growing up Kate engaged with interest in a number of activities. She willingly joined with  neighbors and classmates on sports teams, but they were only a small part of her range of interests. She engaged in adventures and mysteries through books.  Her room showed that she had plenty of heroes because pictures of celebrities were intensely and artistically displayed. She chose her college based on whether if offered opportunities  for freedom of expression, and majored in anthropology. When it came time for getting a job after college, she predictably kept her activities to herself, and decided to develop an interest in clothing for the skateboarding crowd. She read magazines to develop her interest, and initiated contact about job possibilities with the companies who advertised there. Without being specific, she expressed an interest in being involved. After months of interacting, she landed her first job in marketng. After a few years, she focused on a major clothing retailing firm, and after many months of reaching out, listening, and building her interests landed an executive track job.*

Sometimes we spend so much time in endeavors we "should do" but for which we have no real joy that we lose sense of where our true interests lie. We bury them as we do our best to handle what we must. However to find work that matches our interests, we must know what they are. Your interests can be seen in your favorite hobby and in what you do on your day off. They can be seen through what spontaneously jumps into your mind when it is idle. They can be seen in what you dream about doing.

Taking an interest inventory such as the one at www.CareerKey.org will suggest some themes showing what your interests are. It will also suggest compatible occupations. To make the feedback more beneficial you need to integrate the information into the way you see yourself.

The following chart provides an opportunity to do that by comparing the actions from your STARS stories with the six major interest themes.

## Actions and Interests

Look at the actions in your stories and place each in the interest category to which it most applies. If you have a strong interest, you will see many actions in one category. Not everyone has a strong interest. In that case, the actions will be spread through all themes.

| Realistic<br>Ex: Working with tools | Intellectual<br>Ex: Seeking new knowledge | Artistic<br>Ex: Appealing to sensitivities |
|---|---|---|
| Social<br>Ex: Forming relationships | Enterprising<br>Ex: Risking to get reward | Conventional<br>Ex: Carrying out procedures |

# ABILITIES AND KNOWLEDGE

In our daily work, our family, social, and civic activities, and our hobbies, we demonstrate a large number of abilities. When we need to, we can do a great variety of tasks at an acceptable level. If our boss asked us to research vendors and initiate relationships, we could do it. If we had to sell something in a pinch, we could become very persuasive. If we had to increase quality or make procedures more efficient, we would find a way. We often teach someone something we are not experts at and are able to counsel a friend if needed.

For the abilities that will drive our career, however, we need some important information:

- To engage successfully in an occupation, we need to know how our abilities relate to what it requires.

- To contribute immediately and meaningfully to our work, we need to be aware of our skills and knowledge.

- To make a decision about career direction, we need to know the abilities, skills, and knowledge areas we most readily learn.

- To succeed in a career, we need to do some things in a superior way. We need to know what we do best.

- In our work, we need to perform some tasks continually. We need to know what we are able to do well repeatedly, without undergoing stress that will reduce our effectiveness over time.

### Using High- and Medium-Level Abilities

*Although Charlie knew his strength lay in his ability to influence people and he had a great sense of humor, his goal upon graduating from a university with a Speech Communications major did not necessarily tie into those talents. He simply wanted to get the best job he could. He found a position as a customer service help person for a Unix software applications company, and he was successful because of his customer-oriented personality and his learning how to solve Unix software problems.*

*He had confidence that he could learn whatever a job required—his medium-level ability, his adaptability—even if it did not match his best ability.*

*When he wanted to make more money and was able to take on the risk of having some dry months, he moved to a sales position with an Internet marketing company. Charlie now works in a different, more competitive sales position and is successful because he is working in the area of his best abilities and because he knows that he can learn whatever ability he needs to be successful in the situation.*

To deploy abilities effectively we need to practice them, and when practice has created proficiency, the ability becomes a skill. In some cases, when we stop using a skill, such as in riding a bicycle, we need only a little bit of practice to return to our original level of proficiency. Other skills, such as performance-level piano playing, take lots of practice both to achieve mastery and to maintain that level. For most people, many occupational abilities, such as active listening, decline after about a year without practice. Thus, we must know when a new challenge at work will require immediate skill in order to plan ramp up practice time. It's important to recognize that with practice we can regain even our most underutilized skills—if we performed effectively in the past, we can tap into the same skills to do just as well in the future.

Knowledge forms a part of our abilities. Most of what we do requires knowledge about something. Product-development work might require the knowledge of a scientific discipline. Information-technology work requires knowledge of programming languages and platforms. Providing counseling requires knowledge of some theories on people's inner workings. A manager handling a sensitive interpersonal situation requires knowledge of the effectiveness of a participatory management style. The knowledge that job applicants have about key people in an industry may determine who gets hired to fill a sales position.

Our beliefs about our abilities impact our confidence in approaching new career situations. We have the right to feel confident that we have a large number of potential abilities because we have performed many diverse activities in the past. Some of our abilities stand out more than others because we used them frequently and effectively; others because they took advantage of one of our intelligences; and still others because acquired knowledge enhanced what we did.

As we increase our abilities, we build confidence for approaching new career situations as well as make ourselves more attractive to potential employers. Advancing in our career or finding a position that better matches our personality requires adding to our store of abilities. We have many means at our disposal for continuing to grow in this way—engaging in new experiences, practicing the skills we do have to perfect them, entering educational programs, and more.

To begin to understand your abilities, ask yourself what you did to accomplish your career goals to date. Look at what natural abilities you have that helped you to create results that you value. Think of a time when you developed an ability that did not come naturally.

ONET, the career search system sponsored by the US Department of Labor, provides a skill search that enables career seekers to select their developed skills and see the occupational categories that use them. It lists thirty-five skills in six categories—basic, complex problem-solving, resource management, social, systems, and technical—and highlights those that are in demand. To take this quick and extremely useful inventory, go to http://online.onetcenter.org/skills/. The ONET system is a valuable resource for people at all stages of their career and job search. Taking this skills inventory will also give you a list of potential occupations with links to further information for each one.

### Actions and Capacity Development

Look at your actions again to learn about the development of your capacities. Place a check next to the one each action most clearly demonstrates.

| | |
|---|---|
| Physical | |
| Emotional | |
| Intellectual | |
| Non-physical or Spiritual | |

# ORGANIZATIONAL SUPPORT DESIRES

We won't be at our best unless we feel at home in and supported by the environment in which we are working. Some people thrive in competitive arenas, feel restrained in different environments. Some people come alive when they are outdoors but wilt if they are forced to work behind a desk. Some love the challenge of handling crisis after crisis while others prefer calm and quiet to accomplish their tasks.

Here are different types of support we can have in an organization, each with an example of a job or industry which commonly uses it:

- Independent – flexible environment regarding lifestyle and interests, such as at an advertising agency
- Consistent – stable and predictable industry without much innovation, such as the utilities industry
- Varied – challenges in the job never let up, such as in handling customer-service problems every day
- Competitive – achievement depends upon how others do relative to your own performance, such as in a high-stakes sales environment
- Structured – work that follows a spelled-out protocol, such as in the insurance industry, which must comply with rules
- Team-oriented – consensus for decisions and cooperation in meeting goals, such as in many large companies
- Project-oriented – a sense of urgency that motivates many, such as in a software company
- Status-based – well-known or high-profile company, a leader in its industry, such as Microsoft for software design
- Friendly – positive interpersonal relationships, such as in a nonprofit organization for cancer survivors
- Results-oriented – tangible evidence of employees' efforts, such as a completed office building

Today, companies realize that their survival depends on the innovative thinking of their employees, and they have created unique environments to attract the people they need. In turn, we realize that our best performance relates to the environment in which we work, and we will search for companies that have created the ones that play to our uniqueness and bring out our best.

### Job Environment Fit

*Roger's most valued possession was his independence. He had ideas about how things could improve, and goals to create something innovative, and he had little patience with organizations that required regimentation. His first success was working for himself in designing a software product to manage building maintenance. He gambled that his alternative views were what was needed in difficult environmental projects and decided to attend graduate school. His intuition proved correct. After graduation, his history in creating an environment that stimulated alternative thinking was the reason he was hired to lead a government contractor doing research and environmental remediation for a nuclear facility.*

When we are walking around a city, looking for a fun place to go for an evening out, we look in the windows of a number of places. We may notice the decor on the walls, the furniture, the types of people, and whether they are enjoying themselves. We quickly get an overall feel for the atmosphere of the place. Our decision on whether to stay draws on both our interests and our abilities. For instance, we may want to meet certain kinds of people, and we may want to hear specific kinds of music, both of which help narrow down our choices. Sometimes a large part of our satisfaction at work comes from the environment in which we carry it out. In considering our priority competencies, it's important to look at the environment in which they are usually employed and to select one that stimulates and supports our best work.

Ask yourself some questions to get an idea of the atmosphere in which you can perform at your highest level:

- Think about a time when you were performing at your best, not just at work but at any time in your life. What type of environment surrounded you then? What did people say to you or do with you? What did the place look like—a few or many people, open area or separate cubicles, chaos or order?

- When have you felt supported and happy with your work environment so that you performed at your best? What element of that environment made the most significant contribution to how you felt?

- In the preceding list of different types of support, which one or ones do you most want in your work environmental?

- Which do you most want to avoid?

A job "fits" when it satisfies all of a person's career choice factors. In the following example, the six career choice factors we are using are underlined.

### Characteristics Combine into Competencies

*Sam was working as a teacher, a situation which matched his career choice factors. When he looked at a situation calling for his teaching talent, his energy and <u>preferences</u> brought his attention to supporting positive change in the pupil. His kind of <u>intelligence</u> enabled him to use interesting stories with analogies when he was explaining ideas. One of his favorite things to do was to interact with people about learning, and this <u>interest</u> motivated him to research new teaching methods in his spare time. He had developed <u>abilities</u> to implement many effective teaching methods and could successfully and skillfully draw on these and his extensive <u>knowledge</u> bank when needed. Teaching filled his <u>need</u> for contact with people and fulfilled his valued result of helping people to live more productive lives. A school was a <u>supportive environment</u> for him, and he felt* *that he could fulfill his potential there surrounded by other teachers, and students. Sam noticed that he felt creative, enthusiastic and physically energized when teaching, and he never tired of doing it. His life felt meaningful.*

Sam has a competency in teaching. It combines his priorities in all of the six choice points we have considered.

In this chapter we have improved our understanding of our most important career characteristics.

- Which of the career choice factors discussed in this chapter—values and needs, intelligences, preferences, interests, supportive environment desires, and abilities and knowledge—has been a source of satisfaction in former jobs?

- Which characteristic has been a reason why you disliked a former job?

- What is your biggest motivator now?

## CHAPTER FOUR

# CONNECTING WITH COMPETENCY STORIES

We have learned that before we can move forward, we must first understand our past. To discover the place where we will carry out our best work, we examined our performance in previous situations in the areas of work as well as play, school, and more. We have looked at some stories of our accomplishments and the actions in them. These actions have been the expression of our career themes in the areas of our values, intelligences, preferences, interests, environmental support desires, and abilities. Our goal now is to put this information together to open up options for our future career path.

The stories and actions we have identified lie along our career path up to now. To see options for where our path can lead in the future, we can use the same method almost all medium and large sized organizations use to hire, manage, and develop their employees: identifying competencies. In this method, actions that excellent employees take are grouped into clusters and given names. They appear in job descriptions, job announcements, and personal development plans. When we seek to manage the direction of our career path we can use the same method and build on our foundation of competencies. We can identify our excellent actions, group them into clusters, give them competency names, and compare our competencies to those required for success on a job. In our career communications we can highlight our priority competencies. To improve our performance we can develop new competencies and partner when needed to bring new expertise to our efforts to create impactful results.

Previous methods of matching people with jobs involved researching to identify constructs that properly described people, creating tests to identify the extent to which an individual possessed those constructs, and studying jobs to identify which constructs they needed. These methods assumed that one true system worked for all, and it strove to understand which parts of the system applied to the current situation and to make a match. The process was time consuming, limiting, and difficult to apply. It also overlooked some obvious ways to link people reliably and validly to jobs.

David McClelland, a psychologist and Harvard professor, had conducted widely recognized work in motivation, which led to his interest in implementing a job analysis and selection process that organizations could use to insure that people with the most matching motivations and other characteristics were selected for jobs.[1] Because of his research and findings, the State Department retained him in 1973 to identify the best candidates for Foreign Service jobs. The method in use at the time selected candidates who had high IQ scores and had attended prestigious colleges or universities. His job analysis, instead, looked at what the job really required. Because research had proven that people could effectively report on actions that they had observed, he asked Foreign Service workers who were already successful to identify actions that their outstanding co-workers took that resulted in above average performance. Next, from a pool of candidates, he identified those who had successfully demonstrated those needed actions. The candidates he hired were more successful than those hired using the old method.

A major benefit in McClelland's method is the flexibility in its analysis, which results in capturing performance traits that don't always fit preconceived ideas. For instance, coaches and players long assumed that a football quarterback had ability either in dropping back in the pocket for an accurate pass in a predictable way or in scrambling in order to inject unpredictability into a play and spontaneously take advantage of opportunities as they arose. However, Ben Roethlisberger has a different ability. He identifies the best time to stay in the pocket and the best time to roll out and scramble. Under the old assumptions, Roethlisberger would not make a good draft pick because he lacked a high score in either of the traditional performance categories. Only when we put aside old assumptions do we leave room to see new, better opportunities. Only when we set aside limiting ideas about what makes excellent performance on the job and look with fresh eyes do we make accurate choices on the best candidates for the work.

Looking at what people do in a job that makes them effective can result in some surprises. Many people think that it's most important for a sales person to speak effectively about a product. But competency studies have shown that good listening skills result in better sales performance; asking questions gets others talking about their needs so the sales person can fit his or her presentation to address those expressed requirements.

Effective performance depends on the specifics of a situation. Success in project management in one organization may look different from that in another. A person who sells one product successfully may fail at selling another. A manager whose participative style succeeds in one organization may fail in another with a different culture.

The competency methodology will help you to carry out the most important aspect of a career and job search—to identify and talk about the actions that you like and do well—because they will lead you to the position that best matches fulfilling work for you.

### New Options through Competencies

*Initially, Matt managed sports for a youth organization. Looking for a better paying position, he parlayed his skills in handling customer relationships into building management and retaining tenants for a commercial real estate firm. He successfully used his abilities to deal with people and achieved a good record of meeting the many needs of the tenants and retaining them as lessees.*

*Matt again felt the need to move forward with his career but did not know the direction to take. Turning to the competency methodology, he identified all of his effective actions, recognizing that he could combine them in any of various ways to find a suitable match in work. Some of the actions Matt articulated from looking at all of the actions in his related previous experiences included seeing others' priorities, valuing others' points of view, forming relationships with a variety of people, appealing to others' interests, engaging in games such as fantasy sports, noticing when others were dissatisfied, and having fun with friends.*

*These could be combined into a number of competencies, including one called Responding to Expectations. He could talk about this competency with the management of a sports team and, in a brainstorming-like session, help the person see the need for a person like him in its marketing organization. Further, he could help the people in the sports organization to see that there is opportunity in forming online interest communities, beginning with fantasy teams. He would then be in a position to help them create a job that would be new to the organization, with himself as the ideal candidate for it.*

## COMPETENCY METHODOLOGY

The underlying principle of competencies is that consistent actions account for excellent and above average performance on specific jobs. This combines with the belief that there are individuals who have a unique combination of characteristics that make them exceptional in carrying out those actions on those jobs.

To discover competencies required for a particular job, organizations first identify their above-average and excellent performers. Then they ask them to describe in story from what they and their work mates do to create outstanding results. Those using this process identify a large number of actions, group them according to commonalities, and then give the groups meaningful names.

Here is a story about an above-average performance by an IT project manager, as told by one of his fellow managers.

> *We were in the planning stages of a large project which consisted of sub-projects that had to be completed on time. The project manager made an analysis of the strengths and weaknesses of the employees on his team. In talking about them, he mentioned their personality habits that would help and those that might get in the way. He also considered changing the role assignments to minimize problems of personal incompatibility. This required quite a bit of understanding about the kinds of interface that would happen in the future. Because of his positive relationships with the other managers, his ideas were adopted and used by others, improving the performance of the whole department.*

Companies in search of talent look for individuals who tell stories similar to the ones told about their above-average employees. Here is Ted's story, which would impress a company looking to fill a project manager position similar to the one in the above story.

> *I was in my late twenties, and I wanted to improve my ability to talk to the customers I would have in a new job. A friend suggested I join Toastmasters, and I did. Mainly, I wanted to improve my ability to listen and to think fast on my feet. After completing some successful speeches, I decided to go for some bigger challenges. When the speech contest came up, I took a chance and entered, even though I was still a relative rookie. I identified a topic I thought people in the audience could identify with, which was how to fail at picking up a woman. I had a few humorous*

*examples from my own experiences and had spoken with my friends about this topic frequently enough so that I had some of theirs as well. During the speech, I carefully observed the reaction of the audience and adjusted my timing accordingly. In the end, everyone laughed a lot and, of course, voted for me.*

Employers select a person for a job by finding commonalities in the stories the applicant tells with the stories they have developed for that position; they look for similar actions. Both of the previous two stories describe a person who has an understanding of the uniqueness of people and who successfully tailors communication to others' sensitivities.

Can you see, too, how people would tend to remember Ted's story? Its specificity and detail has far greater impact than just saying, "I joined Toastmasters to improve my speaking ability in public." The sequence of this story, from a situation, to intention, to actions, and to results, forms a complete unit. It creates a pattern and holds a special place in the brain, and so the listener easily remembers it—as well as Ted, who told it. It conveys his uniqueness. Ted selected an interesting topic, designed a speech from the point of view of other people, and showed his sense of humor. Ted is expressing his uniqueness. No other person has carried out an experience like this in exactly the same way. Others have given speeches, others have entered speech contests, others have told funny stories. But no one else has done those things with the added dimensions of Ted's story—where he took a chance and read his listeners and adapted his actions based on what he saw.

People's most competent actions combine all of their career choice factors that we discussed in the last chapter—values, intelligences, preferences, interests, environmental support desires, and abilities. They give a clear picture of who they are and how they would perform in another job, as well as demonstrate their ability to achieve success. They show how superior results have been achieved because they worked to satisfy a strong internal need based on certain values. They show a person learns through the unique way he or she approached the inherent problems. The person related to the task in some way and found it interesting to perform. In the end, the actions illustrate what the person would do in similar situations, which a potential employer wants to know.

The following chart shows some of the competency labels that organizations commonly use.

## Competency Names in Common Use[2]

| Self | Physical | Emotional | Intellectual | Non-Physical |
|---|---|---|---|---|
| Endurance | Physical Endurance | Teamwork | Critical Thinking | Strategic Thinking |
| Integrity | Results Focus | Communication | Systems | Creativity |
| Value Diversity | Monitoring | Influence | Modeling | Out of the Box Thinking |
| Awareness | Organization | Developing Others | Financial Understanding | Innovation |
| Learner | Process Efficiency | Market Knowledge. | Depth of Thinking | Vision |
| Commitment to Quality | Efficiency. | Political Savvy | Diagnostic Focus | Planning |
| High Standards | Entrepreneurship | Customer Focus | Tactical Expertise | Insight |
| Strong Ego | Optimizing Re-sources | Leadership | Conceptual | Foresight |
| Action | Action Bias | Caring | Analytical | Anticipating Events |
| Proactive | Seizing Opportunities | Conflict Management. | Developing. Theories | |
| Decisive | Practical Thinking | Alliances | Information Seeking | |
| Self-control | Concern for Order | Team Leadership | Technical Expertise | |
| Resistance to Stress | | Empathy | Knowledge Use | |
| Calmness | | Sensitivity | Pattern Recognition | |
| Confidence | | Impact | | |
| Flexibility | | Collaboration | | |
| Resilience | | Showmanship | | |
| Balance | | Organizational Tact | | |
| | | Relationships | | |
| | | Working through Others | | |
| | | Rapport | | |
| | | Use of Power | | |

Competency names have different meanings in different companies. For instance, actions related to superior customer service in a software supplier will not exactly match those in customer service for an appliance-repair company.

## CLUSTERING ACTIONS INTO COMPETENCIES

The STARS format used to expand your key experiences in Chapter 2 added an essential specificity to your recollection of the past. Your memory of each experience went from a title and a general impression to a rich description. The next step is to look at all of the elements in your STARS stories to identify the actions that showed your abilities and interests. These actions will form the basis for your competencies. Actions can be something you did that could be directly seen, something you felt or thought that could not be directly observed but that stood behind your outward actions, or knowledge that you used.

Jenny was an early-thirties, single woman with an AA degree who wanted to take the right next career step. Her work experiences included selling text books and as well as functioning as a team leader for other sellers, being program manager of a university research project, practicing as a massage practitioner, and working in a university facilities office. From these experiences and from her hobby of traveling, she wrote seven stories.

In the following STARS Stories Actions table, the title of each of her seven stories appears in boldface at the top. Then many of the actions that she and her reviewing partner saw in her STARS stories are listed. Follow this model to do the same thing. Enter the titles of your seven key STARS stories that you expanded in Chapter 2 in the table on Page 75 or onto a sheet of paper with similar boxes. Then reread your stories and list all of the actions that can be seen in each one. Doing this activity with a partner usually results in identifying more actions than you would discover on your own. This is an opportunity to recall the experience again and identify many of actions that you enjoyed and that helped to create the result. At this point, list every action you can think of, even though it was a small part of the experience and even though you might not think that you liked doing it or were very good at it.

Enter the number of the story in front of each action. This enables you to see where the action originated in the next step in which the actions are clustered.

## STARS Story Actions – Jenny's Example

| 1 - Leading a motivational meeting for a sales team | 2 - Appreciating cultures in China |
|---|---|
| 1 - Being an example of an upbeat person | 2 - Reading travel literature |
| 1 - Getting the attention of a group | 2 - Watching people |
| 1 - Using voice to create emphasis | 2 - Appreciating other cultures |
| 1 - Putting ideas in order | 2 - Learning history |
| 1 - Saying things that attract attention | 2 - Understanding different viewpoints |
| 1 - Persuading doubtful people | 2 - Identifying with acting out of a religious belief |
| 1 - Thinking on my feet | 2 - Knowing what being humble feels like |
| 1 - Putting body language with words | 2 - Being spiritually connected |
| 1 - Explaining techniques | 2 - Seeing patterns in art |
| **3 - Designing a data tracking system** | **4 - Performing a healing massage** |
| 3 - Understanding importance of collecting accurate data | 4 - Perceiving how a person feels from his or her appearance |
| 3 - Seeing the big picture | 4 - Projecting a healing attitude |
| 3 - Dividing things into categories | 4 - Feeling through hands |
| 3 - Attending to detail | 4 - Using empathy to draw people out |
| 3 - Understanding statistics | 4 - Putting symptoms together into a pattern |
| 3 - Using technology | 4 - Projecting calmness and presence |
| 3 - Double checking | 4 - Saying the right thing at the right time |
| 3 - Observing for accuracy | |
| **5 - Participating in a discussion in history class** | **6 - Keeping current on alternative healing techniques** |
| 5 - Feeling strongly about an idea | 6 - Reading and comprehending |
| 5 - Understanding commonalities and differences | 6 - Following leads |
| 5 - Wanting to speak up | 6 - Organizing knowledge systematically |
| 5 - Standing my ground | 6 - Visioning possibilities |
| | 6 - Understanding a variety of ideas |
| | 6 – Having curiosity for inspiring ideas |
| | 6 - Investigating and digging |
| **7 - Helping a research leader solve a problem.** | |
| 7 - Listening to complicated explanations | |
| 7 - Questioning to bring out facts | |
| 7 - Thinking logically and deeply | |
| 7 - Understanding statistical models | |

After you list the actions from your stories, cluster them into competencies. The way Jenny clustered her actions is shown in the table below. Use the Competency Groupings worksheet on Page XX or a paper with the same kinds of boxes to cluster your actions into competency groups.

1.  Looking through all of your actions, select the one you feel most strongly about wanting to use in the future. Write it in the first box. This is your best estimate or guess about your interests and values at this time. If you have a passion about doing something, you will feel it here because you have not combined it with, or hidden it among, other actions, which may not have the same intensity. This is the beginning of a process that moves from feeling strongly about your actions, to prioritizing your competency groupings, to reality testing your views through researching, to selecting a target occupation, to selecting the ideal next role for you, and finally to selecting work. Even if you do get a strong feeling here, it may change as your self -understanding increases through all of these steps.

2.  Find similar actions in the other experiences and put them in the same box. As the additional actions are included, you will get a deeper view of what really motivates you. Place a check next to the actions you take from the STARS Story Actions sheet so that you do not select an action twice.

3.  Next, look for an action that was completely different, and put it in the next box. Search for similar actions to join it in the box, and get a clear view about what the crux of that cluster of actions is.

4.  Proceed to find additional actions that bring out your motivations, place them in the other boxes, and find supporting actions to join them.

5.  Work at distributing and redistributing the actions until you have identified eight competency groupings. You are learning flexibility of thinking, shaking your categories up. You

might need to move some actions around because some new groups have been created. Don't worry if at the end you still have actions that are not in their ideal place. We are learning flexibility. This activity gets at the core of your choosing and decision making and is a good view into what will make your career go forward in a strong way.

6.   Read the actions in each grouping to create a competency designation for many of the actions you are seeing in each group. You might be able to identify a phrase that goes beyond the short phrases which are commonly used to describe ability areas. A large number of phrases are possible, and your work here is a valuable step towards verbalizing your uniqueness.

At this point, it's wise to create competency phrases that can be used in a number of occupations and industries. In the example, Jenny could have specified that her experiences and interests included "presenting and interpreting health care ideas." But she postponed including health care in her competencies because her goal for career searching in this exercise was to discover a number of industries in which she could present and interpret ideas.

Pay attention to all eight competency descriptions, even those at the bottom of the list. They all describe what motivates you and what you do well, and may prove valuable in a future occupational role.

# Competency Groupings – Jenny's Example

(The numbers to the left of each phrase refer to the story number. Competency names are in boldface at the bottom)

| | | | |
|---|---|---|---|
| 5 - Feeling strongly about an idea | 6 - Visioning possibilities | 4 – Using empathy to draw people out | 2 - Appreciating other cultures |
| 5 - Standing my ground | 4 - Putting symptoms together into a pattern | 4 - Perceiving how a person feels from his or her appearance | 2 - Learning history |
| 2 - Understanding different viewpoints | 3 - Seeing the big picture | 2 - Knowing what being humble feels like | 2 - Being spiritually connected |
| 6 - Understanding a variety of ideas | 2 - Seeing patterns in art | | |
| 7 - Thinking logically and deeply | 6 – Having curiosity for inspiring ideas | | |
| 1 - Using voice to create emphasis | | | |
| 4 - Saying the right thing at the right time | | | |
| **Speaking persuasively to support an idea** | **Connecting items into new possibilities** | **Having awareness of others and empathy** | **Having cultural sensitivity and understanding** |
| 3 - Observing for accuracy | 7 - Questioning to bring out facts | 1 - Saying things that attract attention | 3 - Understanding importance of collecting accurate data |
| 3 - Attending to detail | 2 - Watching people | 6 - Reading and comprehending | 3 - Understanding statistics |
| 6 - Investigating and digging | 5 - Wanting to speak up | 4 - Projecting a healing attitude | |
| | 7 - Listening to complicated explanations | 5 - Understanding commonalities and differences | |
| **Handling process design and oversight** | **Coordinating and interacting** | **Presenting and interpreting ideas** | **Discussing research ideas and design** |

**STARS Story Actions**

(List actions carried out in each story preceded by the story number.)

| Story # 1: | Story # 2: | Story # 3: | Story # 4: |
|---|---|---|---|
| Story # 5: | Story # 6: | Story # 7: | |

## Competency Groupings

(Group similar actions and give them a competency name.)

| | | | |
|---|---|---|---|
| Competency Name: | Competency Name: | Competency Name: | Competency Name: |
| Competency Name: | Competency Name: | Competency Name: | Competency Name: |

## PRIORITIZING COMPETENCIES

This section provides an opportunity to establish your priorities considering all of your competency clusters. In the following activity, you will compare each of the competencies to every other one and make a decision about which is most important to you. You will picture yourself doing something in comparison to doing something else, sense what you are feeling, and select the competency which you most enjoy using. You will do this twenty-eight times. At the end, you will have a stronger sense about who you are and what is most important to you.

Write each competency grouping you have identified on the lines of the Prioritizing Competencies Grid that follows, one competency per line. Then compare each of your eight top competencies to each other using the numbers on the grid. Starting at the upper left of the grid, compare competency #1 to #2. Go along the diagonal by next comparing #2 and #3. Continue until each one has been compared to every other one. Going along the diagonal enables you continually to compare different competencies. If, instead, you complete the grid by going vertically you will compare the same one competency in succession to others and tend not to pay attention, getting into a habit that could hide your priorities.

Put yourself into the situation and feeling of using each competency so that you select the one you feel strongest about using in the future. For example, in comparing #1 and #2, Jenny pictured herself in a specific situation such as arguing a principle in a court room or debating in a history class and imagined herself speaking persuasively to stand up for an idea. She got a positive feeling. She then pictured herself in a specific situation such as reading philosophy or gathering ideas in researching a topic and imagined herself connecting items into new possibilities. She got a positive feeling. She then compared the intensity of the feelings, made a choice, and circled the matching number on the grid.

After you have finished making all of the comparisons and choices, count your circled numbers and place the total on the lines at the bottom, starting with the ones on the left and ending with the eights on the right.

In Jenny's sample grid, which follows, her eight competency groupings are listed in the top part.

**Prioritizing Competencies Grid – Jenny's Example**

1. ___Speaking persuasively to support an idea___
2. ___Connecting items into new possibilities___
3. ___Having awareness of others and empathy___
4. ___Having cultural sensitivity and understanding___
5. ___Handling process design and oversight___
6. ___Coordinating and interacting___
7. ___Presenting and interpreting ideas___
8. ___Discussing research ideas and design___

**Prioritizing Competencies Grid – Jenny's Example**

Jenny compared each competency group to every other one using the chart. She preceded along the diagonal and made a choice about her strongest motivations, which are bolded and underlined here. She then totaled the choices for each numbered competency. The highest number indicates her priorities at this time.

$\underline{\boldsymbol{1}} - 2$

$\underline{\boldsymbol{1}} - 3 \quad 2 - \underline{\boldsymbol{3}}$

$1 - \underline{\boldsymbol{4}} \quad 2 - \underline{\boldsymbol{4}} \quad \underline{\boldsymbol{3}} - 4$

$\underline{\boldsymbol{1}} - 5 \quad 2 - \underline{\boldsymbol{5}} \quad \underline{\boldsymbol{3}} - 5 \quad \underline{\boldsymbol{4}} - 5$

$\underline{\boldsymbol{1}} - 6 \quad 2 - \underline{\boldsymbol{6}} \quad 3 - \underline{\boldsymbol{6}} \quad 4 - 6 \quad 5 - \underline{\boldsymbol{6}}$

$1 - \underline{\boldsymbol{7}} \quad \underline{\boldsymbol{2}} - 7 \quad 3 - \underline{\boldsymbol{7}} \quad \underline{\boldsymbol{4}} - 7 \quad 5 - \underline{\boldsymbol{7}} \quad 6 - \underline{\boldsymbol{7}}$

$\underline{\boldsymbol{1}} - 8 \quad \underline{\boldsymbol{2}} - 8 \quad \underline{\boldsymbol{3}} - 8 \quad \underline{\boldsymbol{4}} - 8 \quad \underline{\boldsymbol{5}} - 8 \quad 6 - \underline{\boldsymbol{8}} \quad 7 - \underline{\boldsymbol{8}}$

Total 1: _5_ 2: _2_ 3: _4_ 4: _6_ 5: _2_ 6: _3_ 7: _4_ 8: _2_

## Prioritizing Competencies Grid

Identify your top eight competency groupings and list them below.

1._____

2._____

3._____

4._____

5._____

6._____

7._____

8._____

## Prioritizing Competencies Grid

Compare each action to every other action using the chart. Proceed along the diagonal and circle the preferred competency. Then total the circles for each competency. This prioritization greatly increases the focus and energy you will bring to your work finding activities.

```
1 – 2
1 – 3  2 – 3
1 – 4  2 – 4  3 – 4
1 – 5  2 – 5  3 – 5  4 – 5
1 – 6  2 – 6  3 – 6  4 – 6  5 – 6
1 – 7  2 – 7  3 – 7  4 – 7  5 – 7  6 - 7
1 – 8  2 – 8  3 – 8  4 – 8  5 – 8  6 – 8  7 – 8
Total  1:___ 2:___ 3:___ 4:___ 5:___ 6:___ 7:___ 8:___
```

## *FROM PRIORITIZING TO NEW OPTIONS*

Many people assume that increased prioritizing leads to fewer options. If anything is possible, there must be a lot of possibilities, they reason. But the opposite is true. The more you prioritize, the more options you will see. In finding your work, the first step is to prioritize your competencies. The priority competency you identified in the previous activity is the strongest expression that you are able to verbalize at this time about who you are and what you want to do.

The following chart provides a listing of actions and related occupations I developed. It consists of eight groups of actions and related occupations. Each group is a combination of one of the four functions identified by Jung combined with a preference for bringing information in, Introversion, or sending information out, Extraversion.

Look at the competency you identified as your priority, and select the grouping which is most similar. Then review the approximately 15 actions that are typical of that group, and notice the occupation in which each action is important and frequently performed. You may have developed competency in those activities. Those occupations may be possibilities for you.

| **Introverted Sensing** | Applying detail | Accountant |
|---|---|---|
| | Analyzing thoroughly | Actuary |
| | Investigating completely | Applied Scientist |
| | Observing details | Auditor |
| | Seeing what is practical | Complaint Person |
| | Observing closely | Construction |
| | Reviewing detail | Superintendant |
| | Creating art in objects | Contract Administrator |
| | Working to exact standards | Craft Worker |
| | Organizing data | Dentist |
| | Upholding standards | Research Data Worker |
| | Repeating routine | Educational Administrator |
| | Following procedures | Farming |
| | Caring one on one | Government Administrator |
| | Applying rules | Health Care Worker |
| | Considering individual likes | Insurance Underwriter |
| | Delving deeply into info. | Interior Decorator |
| | Following exact | Library Researcher |
| | measurements | Pharmacist |
| | Tracking details | Project Manager |
| | Observing accurately | Photographer |
| **Extraverted Sensing** | Living in the moment | Actor |
| | Appreciating appearances | Real Estate Stager |
| | Reacting quickly | Emerg. Med. Tech. |
| | Persisting in activity | Guard |
| | Succeeding with people | Mediator |
| | Problem solving practically | Nurse |
| | Adapting to situations | Performer |
| | Acting resourcefully | Photographer |
| | Troubleshooting effectively | Police Officer |
| | Finding related facts | Maintenance/Repair |
| | Learning from experience | Reporter |
| | Resolving crises | Salesperson |
| | Performing for audience | Social Services Work |
| | | Trip leader |

| | | |
|---|---|---|
| **Introverted Feeling** | Working behind scenes<br>Acting out of conviction<br>Expressing imp. feeling<br>Appreciating quality<br>Enhancing an experience<br>Contributing opinion<br>Working in harmony<br>Sharing personal<br>    experience<br>Approaching flexibly<br>Devotion to a cause<br>Forming relationships<br>Creating a cohesive group<br>Connecting emotionally<br>Expressing an experience<br>Writing creatively | Administrator<br>Advocate<br>Author<br>Finish Carpenter<br>Guide<br>Hair Stylist<br>Program Manager<br>Massage Practitioner<br>Nutritionist<br>Policy Researcher<br>Sales Representative<br>Supervisor<br>Therapist<br>Travel Writer<br>Novelist |
| **Extraverted Feeling** | Collaborating with people<br>Offering pos. feedback<br>Developing rapport<br>Communicating tactfully<br>Coordinating people/events<br>Facilitating conversations<br>Bringing out people's best<br>Initiating relationships<br>Empathizing with feelings<br>Caring for people<br>Creating harmony in<br>    groups<br>Advocating for a cause<br>Evaluating impact on<br>    people<br>Sharing values<br>Expressing feelings<br>Supporting others<br>Helping others reach goals | Association Executive<br>Coach<br>Counselor<br>Diplomat<br>Events planner<br>Executive Manager<br>Fitness Trainer<br>Fundraiser<br>Grief Counselor<br>Long Term Care<br>Marriage Counselor<br>Non-profit Executive<br>Political Staff Worker<br>Religious Worker<br>Services Salesperson<br>Case Worker<br>Supervisor |

| Introverted Thinking | Putting into sequence<br>Devising plans<br>Solving logic problems<br>Examining complex situation<br>Critiquing opinions<br>Seeing efficient solution<br>Selecting best path<br>Interpreting multiple inputs<br>Analyzing data<br>Handling multiple variables<br>Understanding workings<br>Pointing out inconsistencies | Comp. Programming<br>Construction Sup.<br>Detective<br>Ergonomic Investigation<br>Lawyer<br>Manager<br>Network Designer<br>Physician<br>Safety Investigator<br>Securities Analyst<br>Technical Maintenance<br>Economist |
| --- | --- | --- |
| Extraverted Thinking | Sticking to the goal<br>Deciding best course<br>Seeing cause and effect<br>Viewing situation objectively<br>Thinking quickly<br>Getting results<br>Directing people<br>Working efficiently<br>Acting to please<br>Comparing variables<br>Organizing information<br>Working to tight standards<br>Creating efficient path<br>Insuring quality<br>Carrying out ideas | Business Administrator<br>Expeditor<br>Facilities Manager<br>Financial Advisor<br>Manager<br>Manager<br>Military Officer<br>Mortgage Banker<br>Politician<br>Purchasing Manager<br>Researcher<br>Software Architect<br>Systems Analyst<br>Trades Person<br>Engineer |

| **Introverted Intuition** | Understanding assumptions<br>Finding new applications<br>Evaluating programs<br>Forming deep insights<br>Organizing concepts<br>Thinking outside of box<br>Formulating mental models<br>Brainstorming options<br>Seeing possibilities for ideas<br>Creating new frameworks<br>Seeing implications of ideas<br>Learning continuously<br>Creating theory<br>Seeing deep relationships<br>Seeing applications of ideas | Consultant<br>Corporate Trainer<br>Educational Evaluator<br>Futurist<br>Knowledge Manager<br>Market Researcher<br>Mathematician<br>Product Designer<br>Product Manager<br>Program Planner<br>Psychologist<br>Researcher<br>Scientific Researcher<br>Software Architect<br>Strategic Planner |
|---|---|---|
| **Extraverted Intuition** | Generating new ideas<br>Connecting abstract ideas<br>Conveying people potential<br>Planning to use insights<br>Integrating ideas into action<br>Selling point of view<br>Going in new directions<br>Combining multiple sources<br>Imagining new uses<br>Implementing patterns<br>Inspiring with ideas<br>Seeing trends<br>Verbalizing thoughts<br>Initiating change | Advertising Worker<br>Attorney<br>Coach<br>Consultant<br>Entertainer<br>Entrepreneur<br>Explorer<br>Inventor<br>Marketer<br>Mediator<br>Public Relations<br>Social Scientist<br>Teacher<br>Urban Planner |

The competency themes you identify as your priorities will provide a powerful statement about who you are in relation to your career. They will provide the words to make powerful statements on your résumé, in your networking interviews, and in your responses to job interview questions.

With competencies you will be more effective in your work and career search because:

- You will present a fuller, richer person to the potential employer. Rather than restricting yourself to examples from jobs obviously related to the one under consideration, you will give information from a broader range of experiences. You will know where you will contribute the most to your current or potential employer.

- You, the career seeker, will receive affirmation and inspiration in seeing the same words used by an organization to describe excellence in its employees that are also in your dialogue and on your résumé.

- You will find a way to express your true self every day, and in turn be more productive.

- In the process of identifying key experiences from your past, you will have taken the opportunity to look at some of your negative experiences and the related obstacles, and move beyond them.

- As an employee, you will be a pleasure to manage because of your interest in learning more about yourself and in improving.

- You will be rewarded by an upward spiral of improving performance and increasing job satisfaction. You will connect to what is most meaningful to you.

In this chapter we have learned why using competency stories to connect with opportunities in the workplace is a powerful approach. It brings out the unique characteristics of the individual to enable a better comparison with the unique challenges of the job.

- For one of your past jobs, how would using competencies to understand the match between you and the job have made a difference—in knowing what to expect ahead of time, in job satisfaction, in deciding about accepting the job, etc.?

- In thinking of success stories to tell about yourself at work, when you make an effort to think of some of the details, what other details come rushing into your mind?

- When you imagine a desirable future for your career, is it in story form so that you envision doing things and getting successful results, or is it a static picture which you are only hoping for?

## CHAPTER FIVE

# UNIQUE RÉSUMÉ

You are unique. No one has had the same sequence of experiences. No one has had the same accomplishments within those experiences. No one has carried out those accomplishments using the same actions. Crafting your résumé will help you to appreciate your uniqueness, and this is essential for helping you to find your meaningful work and make your work of art. When your resume communicates your uniqueness to your networking contacts, they will have more ideas about where your talents can be used. When your résumé communicates your uniqueness to employers, it helps you stand out. Many employers care more about whether a person is strong and unique than whether he or she has any particular skill. We recommend 6 ways to make your resume unique.

## *PAINT A PICTURE WITH VERB PHRASES*

Companies use the competency method to identify descriptive examples of the excellent work they need. Then they use the examples to develop their job announcements. Your goal is to facilitate a match by using descriptive examples of some of your accomplishments on your résumé. In writing your examples, use words to paint a rich picture of you in action. Employ as many specific action phrases as possible. When the application reviewer reads the action phrases on your résumé, frequently he or she will be reading the same words that are on his or her list describing an ideal candidate, and you will be selected for an interview.

Focus on finding work versus applying for a job will lead you to search for examples of when you were happiest and most effective. You might use an example on your résumé, even if you did not do it very often, because it expresses your best self. Someone who is primarily a job seeker will focus on examples that are impressive to others, regardless of whether they really want to do that kind of thing in the future. A balanced approach is recommended. Always include examples which show times in the past when you have been working at your best. Also include some of your examples which you know will appeal to those who will be reading your résumé.

To write a descriptive example of a past accomplishment that will add power to your résumé, picture yourself in action and then describe it with verb phrases. It's important to use verb phrases rather than a single word. Just using a verb such as "analyze" does not tell the whole story. Analyzing data differs from analyzing the motivations of people. To identify additional words to describe your actions, ask yourself: "What did I do to do that?"

Stories transfer to a résumé with changes to the format. The job title on your résumé communicates your role and something about your situation. Your responsibilities summary communicates what you are trying to do, like a task statement. Your accomplishment bullets present the actions you carried out and the results that you achieved.

## *SHOW-OFF COMPETENCY LEVEL ACTIONS*

Seek to raise the accomplishments on your résumé to the level of competent actions. Competency-level actions are ones that superior performers carry out and average performers do not. These actions ring true with people reading your résumé and add magic to it. Look at what others in your occupation do when they achieve above-average success, look for something similar in your own work history, and include it on your résumé.

**Competency-Level Accomplishment Examples:**

"Increased customer satisfaction by intuiting and acting upon customers' unexpressed needs."

"Identified a large number of possible negative scenarios and prepared a response to each ahead of time, thus completing the project on time and under budget."

"Increased sales by listening to the needs and preferences of prospects and tailoring my presentation to them."

## *Verbalize Your Results*

Sport teams often draft for the best player regardless of his or her position. One reason is that they realize superior performance cannot be easily taught. And this personality characteristic readily transfers to other situations. Research has shown these high-level performers do one thing extremely well: they link their past actions with results. You can do exactly this on your résumé. In writing your examples, pair the verb phrases that describe what you were doing with results.

If you can state your results in objective, quantitative, numeric terms, do so. Providing a number in evidence of your performance increases your credibility because people see numbers as objective and valid. Yes, a result which is from your own point of view and which describes change in quality is also very effective.

**Accomplishment Example with Quantitative Result:**

"Increased sales by 10% by creating new descriptions of the product in action."

**Accomplishment Example with Qualitative Result:**

"Drew out from employees their real opinions about department projects, thus increasing their participation, suggestions, and job satisfaction."

You can begin an effective accomplishment bullet on a résumé with either the action you took to get a result or the result itself. In the preceding, can you identify each? "Identified a large number of possible negative scenarios ..." and "drew out from employees ..." are actions taken. "Increased customer satisfaction ...," "completing the project on time ...," and "increased sales by 10% ..." are all results achieved.

Some résumés focus too much on results, and do not present enough information about how the person achieved those results for the uniqueness of the individual to come out. For example, if you have a good sense of humor, you can convey it on your résumé by using verb phrases.

## MOVE BEYOND PROCLAIMING

Too often people just proclaim in general terms when they talk about themselves rather than giving specific instances of what they did.

**Proclaiming Example:**

"Demonstrated creativity in making sales presentations to prospects."

Proclaiming lacks credibility because of its vagueness. It also detracts from confidence. It draws only from your self-image, which exists in your mind, and it can be difficult to compose as well as validate. Citing an accomplishment, on the other hand, gives a specific instance of what actually happened. It describes a real event, and in writing about it, you go beyond what is in your mind to your memory of the incident. You can much more easily describe an experience than talk about yourself in the abstract. Your describing an accomplishment will actually build your confidence and give support for what you are presenting about yourself.

### Word Picture of an Executive

*Steven had produced impressive results as a leading executive in a manufacturing firm. But his résumé only hinted at his supportive, take-charge attitude and his successes. Although people in his network referred him on to many good opportunities, nothing about his personality came across on paper, and his search for a good position floundered. Steven's résumé lacked specific examples of what he had done to gain success. The people he was meeting could not get a feel for how he would act in their organization because he listed only general terms, such as "worked well with others," "showed initiative," and "achieved success." When asked what he did to have all of those successes, a picture of a person who built strong relationships emerged. Steve's warm mannerism enabled others to accept his decisions and trust that he was working with their best interests when he had to make the tough calls. Now, having incorporated this information into his résumé, he is being referred to situations in which he fits.*

## CREATE A HARD-HITTING PROFILE

Your résumé introduces who you are in your career to others. A résumé with vague or nonexistent priorities or one that tries to be all things to all people presents a fuzzy image, and you will lose your chance to make a memorable impression. Your résumé acts as a reminder of the accomplishments that show why someone should hire you. It needs to stand solidly for something. If it does not state your strong interest in making some kind of impact, no one will retain the information. And you will have lost the opportunity with that organization.

Start your résumé with either a Profile, a Career Summary, or a Qualifications Summary. A Profile shows your passion and specifies the competencies you are most interested in using. (See page 96 for a sample résumé.) This differs from a Career Summary, which reviews past experiences and appears historical. And it differs from a Qualifications Summary, which lists the credentials and years in past jobs that most support your future direction.

For your Profile, include a descriptive phrase that conveys who you are at your core. This is like your "handle." Then indicate what you have a strong interest in and a passion for. Point out your successful experiences, and state some primary areas of expertise. Indicate that you are interested and capable of carrying out other things as well. The reader of your résumé sees a strong person who is able to be effective in a number of areas. With this introduction, he or she looks for supporting evidence in the rest of the résumé. Creating this Profile statement will crystallize your self-understanding and result in increased focus, energy, and creativity. It will not detract from your options because you will be seen as an effective person who has proven that you are able to learn what it takes to succeed.

### Hard Hitting Handle

*Don had a background of many accomplishments in diverse roles and did not believe he could identify one phrase to summarize them all in a way that would convey his purpose. Encouraged to review his key accomplishments again, he saw a theme. "Insightful project planner and implementer with a strong interest in efficient systems" became the first line of his Profile. It described the accomplishments that fit his true career path. He made it specific enough to convey good self-understanding without overly limiting his options. It could apply equally well to the IT area in which he had experience and to other areas of an organization seeking to improve efficiency*

## ALIGN SUPPORTING EXPERIENCES

The experience which provides the best support for the direction stated in the Profile should follow immediately. If you are a new graduate and your most relevant accomplishments occurred in school, the Education section would come next. If your most recent employment contains your most relevant career accomplishment examples, that experience would come next. If the best experience happened several jobs previously, you have two options. One, the section that the reader sees first in which you describe past jobs could be called Related Experience. This provides permission to adjust the order of how the jobs are presented.

A section called Other Experience would follow, and the jobs that are not directly relevant would be presented there. Or two, you can give a specific name for groups of experiences and include more than one Experience section, each with a different title, in the résumé. The title of the Experience section the reader sees first would provide support for the description and direction stated in the Profile.

> *Roberta had experience as both a fashion designer and an apparel technical designer. She had a stronger interest in fashion design, but her most recent job was as a technical designer. To reflect her preference in positions, she named the section immediately following her Profile "Fashion Design Experience" and put the jobs most related to that there. The next section she called "Apparel Technical Experience." Finally, she also had a section entitled "Other Experience."*

If a person has a large number of past jobs, the résumé will have a choppy appearance. This can be corrected by grouping similar jobs. Give one job title, and list of the relevant companies under that title.

Your past jobs determine the major organization of your résumé and what you did in them provides the majority of the content. One way to present what you did is to describe your job duties and responsibilities. They are similar to the job descriptions of your past jobs, but are greatly summarized on the résumé. Too much description of job duties, some of which can be determined from the job title, makes the résumé appear heavy and boring. Listing duties can give the potential employer an idea of the variety and uniqueness of the jobs, but if they carry no results, just summarize them. Accomplishments matter more, and you want to give focus to that over mere duties.

When writing a résumé, you should always present the real you, maintaining 100 percent honesty. You can take advantage of the flexibility of your résumé, in comparison to a job application form, by expanding upon what you say on an application to increase accuracy in portraying your priority competencies. In this sense, your résumé is your brochure. If you trained new employees, you can add "trainer" to your job title. If you had accomplishments outside of your job description, such as organizing a company party, you can include them. If you have included your travel in the Interests section, you can expand what you say, for instance, to show that you learned about new cultures. You would expand in ways that reinforce the story you are presenting about who you are.

As your career evolves, your priorities will change. As they do, review your past jobs to identify examples that relate to any new career direction. After you determine how you have grown and what your priority competencies are today, go back to your jobs and identify times when you were demonstrating them. As your career progresses, look at your past jobs with new eyes and find examples of when in the past you have been the person you are planning to be in your future.

There are good reasons for going back no more than ten or twelve years in presenting your experiences. But if in your more distant past you have good examples of demonstrating your current priority competencies, you would include the jobs. For example, if part of your story is that you are a team builder as a manager and you were a captain for a high school team, list and expand that experience in your résumé under a section such as Professional Activities and Other Interests.

## RÉSUMÉ RECASTING

To implement the work finding process described in this book, it pays to recast your résumé to fit your purpose. Work finding has three stages—exploration, niche building, and consultant marketing—and each one calls for you to place different information in the top position of the résumé. To explore, put your priority competencies at the top. To build a niche, your professional expertise for the niche you are building belongs in that position. And to market yourself as a consultant, your career highlights that relate to your ability to solve the specific problems of your focus should be in the top position.

The following Competency Rich Résumé implements many of the above suggestions.

- The Profile highlights a strong interest and presents priority competencies.

- For the first job listed, the first bullet summarizes responsibilities. The following bullets use the language of competencies by using descriptive verbs.

- The second bullet starts with verb phrases and ends with a result which is subjective. The third bullet starts with a quantitative result followed by verb phrases.

- Using a Related Experiences section groups related experiences at the top even though there was an intervening job.

- The bullet under Other Experiences conveys unique and varied interests and abilities.

- The bullet under Education brings out an interest.

- The bullet under Professional Activities and Interests lists specifics.

The traditional format of the competency rich resume lends itself to many purposes. It can be used in your networking sessions or it can be combined with a letter of interest in a job application.

The Functional-Chronological Targeted Résumé, on the next page, is adapted to be easily submitted to organizations advertising jobs. The top part of the résumé covers competencies and experiences called for in a job ad. The bottom part follows the chronological format that human resource departments require.

This resume responds to the needs of the job advertiser and also brings out the uniqueness of the work seeker. It is very helpful when it is not possible to include a Letter of Interest in the companies' resume data base. It can also replace the letter to speed up the application process.

- The five competency paragraphs at the top of the resume are targeted to the abilities requested in the advertised job announcement. You would keep a list of twenty to thirty of these paragraphs and reuse them when possible. With this efficiency you will be able to apply to a larger number of job openings.

- The paragraphs contain verb phrases and results. The results are both quantitative and qualitative.

- The fifth competency paragraph contains a description of total selling experience.

- The major work experience is presented in the traditional way HR resume reviewers like to see. Minor work experiences are just listed.

- The bullet in the Education section contains an accomplishment bringing out additional competencies.

- Entries in the Activities and Interests section bring out specific competencies.

*Competency Rich Résumé*

**Steve Bloom**

505 10th Ave, Bellingham, WA, 360-454-9854, jos2009@gmail.com

### Profile

Results-oriented project manager with a strong interest in working through people. Successful experiences improving communication across functional areas to resolve issues. Excellent record of anticipating and resolving issues to expedite production. Skilled facilitator and negotiator.

### Related Experience

**Project Manager**, Technical Laboratories, Inc., Bellingham, WA, 2004–2008

- Responsible for setting up communication processes and tracking systems with milestones to monitor automated manufacturing.

- Projected and perceived potential problem areas and planned response options in advance so that all projects were completed on time and under budget.

- Resolved 60% of clients' concerns in the first meeting by bringing out and listening to their issues and presenting considerations that helped them to see the big picture.

**Design Engineer**, P & E Engineers, Bellevue, WA, 1998 - 2001

- Provided design solutions for a wide range of technical product projects.

- Supported marketing by mocking up demonstration projects, presenting them to potential customers, and answering their questions. This resulted in credibility for our company and successful bids.

### Other Experiences

**Camera and Technical Retail Sales**, Advanced Cameras, Seattle, WA, 2002-2003

- Approached customers, asked questions, demonstrated projects and made sales of cameras and other technical equipment and software.

- Developed a demonstration of video editing software which increased customers' interest in exploring a range of products within our store.

### Education

**BS Mechanical Engineering**, 1995, University of Washington

- Photographer for the Daily newspaper.

### Professional Activities and Interests

Member, Project Management Association: Helped to identify yearly program. Snow Boarding: Developed new tricks.

*Functional-Chronological Targeted Résumé*

**William Green**
250 55th St., Seattle, WA, 206-971-4593, cs2020@yahoo.com

**Marketing.** Developed a marketing plan for a services organization which included print and broadcast media. Utilized focus group research to identify effective, specific messages. Impact was shown by an increase in calls received and a higher closure rate.

**Coaching.** Maximized the personal growth of participants in an educational program by tailoring my style of communication to individuals' unique characteristics. Completion rate in the program was very high. Increased the performance of a sales team by forming relationships, asking questions which brought out opportunities for improvement, and shaping problem solving thinking. Sales increased by 15%.

**Activism.** Maintained in-depth knowledge of land use issues relating to wildlife preservation and communicated with legislators.

**Sales/Influencing/Presentations.** Over 10 years successful experience in sales-oriented situations. History of creativity in influencing individuals and groups. Designed the curriculum and created the graphics for a group presentation which increased motivation for personal financial planning.

### Work Experience

**Account Executive,** Financial Services Corporation, Seattle, WA 2003–2008

- Worked with clients to design financing programs which supported their unique situations. Created and carried out promotional campaigns.
- Improved the closure rate for all of the consultants by listening to questions and writing sample answers.
- Built a reputation for utilizing networking relationships. Business has increased steadily.

Other work experiences: waiter, tutor in college, stagehand for theater, gardener for summer job.

### Education

**BA English**, Seattle University, Seattle, WA, 2000

- Recruited and organized 10 people to present a graduation dinner.

### Activities and Interests

Participant and leader for Forum Training over a 5-year period. Sourced new participants through my enthusiastic networking.

Sierra Club member and participant in land-use activity committees.

As a Big Brother, mentored a teenager to help him complete high school.

This chapter shows that an effective résumé contains a person's past job titles and responsibilities but that the Profile, accomplishments showing results, and the placement of information can greatly impact the impression it makes. Including competency statements on your résumé and arranging items so that they show an aligned purpose can help your true uniqueness to come across.

- What impression do people have of you after reading your current résumé?

- Does your current résumé unnecessarily restrict the way people see you?

- Does your résumé show that your career is proceeding towards a destiny?

## CHAPTER SIX

# EXPANDING PERCEPTIONS

Deepening your knowledge about your self is only part of the challenge of expanding your potential. You need to expend effort to broaden your understanding of the world of work.

You can benefit by opening your eyes to see the bigger work world beyond the narrow confines of your current job and your current perceptions. Looking past the current situation reveals a large number of possibilities. If everything you could know that would help you along your career path were a large circle, what you actually do know is only a dot. Now, imagine the circle full of dots. When explored, each dot is a window that opens to a new world of information that seems to you as large as what you know now.

Your goals in this stage of your career growth are to:

- Expand your awareness of activities in the work world that will take advantage of your competencies.

- Increase your confidence as you successfully meet and interact with people who can help you get the specific information you need.

- Make decisions about where best to utilize your abilities and nourish your interests.

- Identify places where you will find the support you need to move your career forward.

Making decisions about your future requires breaking out of stereotypes, old habits, confining views. Our experiences determine how we see the world, and what we see ignores other perspectives, many of which can hold great potential for us. Our limited view is like having a fence surrounding us where we see only within the confines of that barrier. Going beyond the fence into an open landscape full of opportunities requires first stepping out of one's habitual way of seeing. We all have a map of the work world in our head formed from impacts of the economy on our lives, working at various jobs, learning of others' experiences in jobs, and observing others carrying out economic activities. We use that map to navigate, to make decisions about improving our current job situation, and to make career plans. But any one person in a very large world assuredly has a mental map both incomplete and erroneous.

You explore by opening your eyes, reading written information, and talking with people.

When interacting with sources of new information, you learn new data but do not usually gain new perspective unless you make an extra effort to shed your stereotypes and expand your view. Data goes into your current mental framework, your way of seeing the world. it filters the information, limiting what you can do with it. The extra effort required for expanding your perspective involves questioning yourself so that you are aware of your views before and after reading something. Then, when you encounter information that is different, ask yourself these important questions: What is different? What has taken me by surprise? What am I discovering? How are my assumptions being challenged? What change in beliefs is called for?

### Mind Expanding Researching

*When Richard left his job in finance at a municipality, he knew that he wanted to stay in the same field. He read publications for job ads, but he also read articles carefully to identify financial management issues. He recognized that he had narrow perceptions and attended some professional association meetings in which he met new people who had new ideas. He consciously broadened his perspective by questioning himself as he read. The topic of our discussions was not about the usual concerns, such as communicating with potential employers. Instead, it covered trends and what might be happening so that he could get an advantage on his competition. We did a lot of "what if" thinking. He stepped beyond how he would read as a person in a specific job. Using his imagination, he made an effort to view what he was reading from many perspectives. He used career counseling as an opportunity to get feedback about many of his attitudes and actions. In his interviews he demonstrated an understanding of trends, and this helped him transition into a financial management position for another city.*

## Start with Your Self

The best way to understand needs and possibilities in the work world is to start with yourself.

- What are your most pressing, unfilled needs?
- What is a career direction to fill one of them?
- If you could change something, what would it be?

Many people have used their own needs as motivation to produce inventions and to start successful businesses.

## Look from Different Viewpoints

What you see is unique to you, but it's possible to step into different shoes. As you explore, use the different perspective that each of your capacities brings.

- When looking through your physical capacity, notice the needs for improving the physical living situation and the physical appearance of people. Look for opportunities to improve physical comfort.

- When looking through your emotional capacity, notice the needs of people to be in relationships and to be in experiences that create positive feelings. Look for the opportunities to share positives.

- When looking through your intellectual capacity, notice needs for increasing understanding of how ideas are combined for improvement. Look for opportunities to analyze things and create new knowledge.

- When looking through your non-physical capacity, notice needs to bring something new into existence, possibly through something artistic. Look for opportunities to entertain with ideas.

## OCCUPATIONAL PROJECTIONS

Segments of economic history are called ages, with the primary occupation in that time period part of the name. We have had the Agricultural Age in which the primary occupation was farming, the Industrial Age in which the primary occupation was factory work, and the Information Age in which the primary occupation was knowledge work and information processing. We saw previously that Daniel Pink believes that we are now in the Conceptual Age in which the primary work is creating new ways to use information and using empathy expertly. Richard Florida, author of The Rise of the Creative Class, agrees. He documented the importance of the thirty-five million professionals working in such areas as media, technology, entertainment, and all positions in which creativity adds a needed element. This includes all innovation, as well as work in writing, designing, and art. He goes on to reinforce the idea that the loss of high paying industrial jobs means that everyone must now seek to discover their true creativity and express it through their work. He recommends that workers in service jobs seek to elevate their job by adding their creativity to it. For example, bakers can use their creativity to create healthy and tasty food. People who care for the elderly can invent care methods that will encourage people to pay more for their service.[1]

It's difficult to identify from the numbers alone when one "age" ends and a new one begins. The number of people working in an occupation is so large that a trend does not stand out until years after meaningful change has begun. The occupational projections by the Bureau of Labor Statistics[2] in the following bulleted summary shows that information processing jobs are projected to decline by.4 percent by 2018. Such small changes there and in the other items below, alone, do not show that the Information Age has ended. But recent recessions tell a different story. People are not being hired back into the same office and information processing jobs. Economists theorize that office automation has eliminated those jobs and that employers waited until the recession to eliminate employees.[3]

As of the end of 2009, there were 137 million people working, with an additional 15.3 million, or 10 percent of the total who wanted to work, considered unemployed. The total of those working breaks down into the following categories and percentage of all workers in them. . The predictions for the percentages for 2018 differ only slightly from the 2009 results.

- 22.9 percent worked within physical activities, such as farming, construction, installing, maintaining, repairing, producing, and driving. In 2018 it will be 22.6%.

- 20.6 percent worked in a professional capacity in areas such as information technology, engineering, science, education, law, social service, art, entertainment, and health care. In 2018 it will be 21.8%.

- 20.0 percent worked serving the needs of people as health care assistants, protective service, food service, government service, and tourism. In 2018 it will be 20.2%.

- 16.0 percent worked carrying out support functions for business offices, such as recording, information operating communications equipment. In 2018 it will be 15.6%.

- 10.5 percent worked influencing people in sales and sales related positions. In 2018 it will be 10.2%.

- 10.4 percent worked managing and doing all of the work required to make an organization run. In 2018 it will be 10.5%.

Here are some of the occupations predicted to grow fastest between now and 2018. The percentages are increases in the number of people working in the occupations. Odds of success in changing a career into a growing occupation are higher because you are competing against people who also have little experience.

| | |
|---|---|
| Biomedical Engineers - 72% | Anthropologists/Archeologists - 28% |
| Network and Data Communications Analysts - 54% | Medical Equipment Repairers - 27% |
| Home Health Aides - 46% | Medical Secretaries - 27% |
| Financial Examiners - 41% | Geographers - 26% |
| Medical Scientists - 39% | Cost Estimators - 25% |
| Skin-care Specialists - 38% | Security Alarm Installers - 25% |
| Physical Therapists and Aides - 35% | Environmental Scientists/Geoscientists - 25% |
| Software/Applications Engineers -34% | Civil Engineers - 24% |
| Compliance Officers - 31% | Computer Research Scientists - 24% |
| Environmental Engineers - 31% | Public Relations Specialists - 24% |
| Computer Systems Engineers - 30% | HR/Training Professionals - 24% |
| Nursing, Care, Home Health - 30% | Cargo/Freight Agents - 24% |
| Personal Financial Advisors - 30% | Management Analysts - 24% |
| Fitness Instructors - 29% | Computer Network Administrators - 23% |
| Healthcare Support - 29% | Athletes/Coaches - 23% |
| Market Researchers - 28% | Veterinary Assistants/Animal Lab - 23% |
| HVAC Mechanics - 28% | Social/Human Service Assistants. - 23% |

## COMPARE DATA TO ASSUMPTIONS

Many people assume that occupations that are growing rapidly and pay well require extensive education. But many do not. Check these predictions at the Bureau of Labor Statistics link for fastest growing occupations.[4] It will show you how your assumptions can be wrong. For example:

- Biomedical engineers are the fastest growing group at 72 percent between 2008 and 2018, and only a bachelor's degree is required, and they earn in the highest quartile.

- Financial examiners are the fifth-fastest growing occupation, a bachelor's degree is usually required, and they earn in the highest quartile.

- You may think that a person needs an MD to treat sick people. But physician's assistant, with opportunities expected to grow by 38 percent, the seventh-highest rate, requires only a master's degree, and earnings are in the highest quartile.

- An occupation called athletic trainer exists at the bachelor's level, and it earns in the second highest quartile, whereas Fitness Trainer, also a fast-growing occupation, earns in the lowest quartile.

- You may have assumed that motivational speaking is not an official occupation. But it is listed as the nineteenth-fastest growing group, only work experience is required, and it earns in the second-highest quartile.

- Survey researcher, growing a 30 percent, requires a bachelor's degree and earns in the second-highest quartile.

- Environmental engineering technician is growing at 30 percent, it earns in the second-highest quartile, and it requires only an associate degree.

- Occupational therapy aide is growing at 30 percent but is earning in the lowest quartile, with only on-the-job training required. Occupational Therapy Assistant is also fast growing, requires an associate degree, and earns in the second highest quartile.

## *FIND AND READ ABOUT A VARIETY OF NEW OCCUPATIONS*

Online searching can lead you to new job titles and the information you need to decide whether they are possibilities for you.

Start at http://www.bls.gov/search/ooh.htm and enter the name of an industry or occupation or, even, just a characteristic of a job. You will see a list of occupations and industries with that word or idea. This is mind expanding because the search returns such varied information related to the term. You see a much broader range than possible by paging through written resources. Clicking on one of the items listed connects you to current information for occupations and industries. Here are examples of the large number of jobs and industries related to specific interests or attributes.

- Enter "thorough thinking," and be linked to entries for registered nurses, lawyers, psychologists, science technicians, and computer and information systems managers.

- Enter "empathy in relationships" and be linked to an entry for massage therapists.

- Enter "investigate" and see entries for private detectives, police, science technicians, and accountants/auditors.

- Enter "understand people" and see entries for public relations specialists, psychologists, counselors, and interpreters

- Enter "see things in new ways" and see entries for biological scientists, insurance sales, chemists, lawyers, and trainers.

The site provides the following type of information for the occupations listed:

- Nature of the Work
- Training, Other Qualifications, and Advancement
- Employment
- Job Outlook
- Projected Job Outlook
- Earnings

- Wages
- Related Occupations
- Sources of Additional Information

It provides information in the following categories about the industries:

- Nature of the Industry
- Working Conditions
- Employment
- Occupations in the Industry
- Training and Advancement
- Outlook
- Earnings
- Sources of Additional Information

Savvy business people have developed guides for the most popular occupations. They show what it takes to succeed and present biographies to show how some people prepared themselves. Many jobs in these guides are not listed in government publications. An example can be seen at www.fabjob.com. Do any of the 130 career job titles shown there appeal to you? Do you have stereotypes that prevented you from seeing them? Consider a few from that extensive list that most job seekers would never even think about:

- Social Entrepreneur
- Investigator
- Motivational Speaker
- Food Critic
- Beauty Cream Shop Owner

The site http://www.vocbio.com/indxtseries.htm identifies over 1300 occupations, many of them non-traditional. For three dollars, you can purchase a colorful and thorough four-page guide containing descriptions of an occupation from a number of views, success stories, and ideas about how to get into it. They are also available at employment centers at colleges and state agencies. Information about all traditional occupations you probably have heard about is available. You can also check out little-known occupations such as these. To gain the most from this information, be sure to set aside all prior assumptions about occupations when you read about them.

| | | |
|---|---|---|
| Armorer | Internet Advertising Consultant | Pyrotechnist |
| Braille Proofreader | | Swimming Pool Construction Superintendant |
| Concert Promoter | Jingle Writer | |
| Doula | Lab School Teacher | |
| Ethno Historian | Mystery Shopper | Topiary Artist |
| Family Resource Coordinator | Needs and Services Report Writer | Union Grievance Handler |
| | | Vascular Radiologist |

## INDUSTRY PROJECTIONS

The occupational projections presented previously depict the kinds of work people will be doing in the future. Industry projections depict where they will working. Many occupations work in many different industries, and others work in only a few. Sales people and human resource professionals, for example, work in all industries whereas graphic designers work in only a few.

According to the Bureau of Labor Statistics[5], the following industries will grow in employment by 2018, from highest to lowest growth:

> Professional and Business Services
> Health Care and Social Services
> Educational Services
> Construction
> Leisure and Hospitality

The following industries will decline in employment by 2018, from highest to lowest decline:

Manufacturing
Retail Trade
Wholesale Trade
State and Local Governments
Agriculture and Resources
Financial Activities
Self Employed
Information

The following industries will stay the same:

Transportation and Warehousing
Federal Government

The trend towards most growth in industries requiring creativity and empathy identified by Daniel Pink and Richard Canada mentioned previously can be seen. Within the professional sector, entertainment and environment are high.

## EXPLORE COMPANIES

At http://www.hoovers.com you can enter descriptive words, see companies in the field, and be linked to more information, such as a description of the company its officers, and news and articles. You can also enter job titles.

- Entering "investigate" brought Pinkerton's and nine other companies offering jobs in that area, including a government agency.
- Entering "helping people" brought 239 returns with some interesting companies.
- Entering "artistic expression" brought 11 companies.
- Entering "improving processes" brought 32 companies.

Many more companies can be investigated at http://company. monster.com/. You can search jobs by key word, see the name of the company offering, and locate a description about the company and its career opportunities through the alphabetical browse feature.

## *LOOK AT JOBS OF THE FUTURE*

Many of the work opportunities that prospered in the past have completely disappeared or have few opportunities and are gradually shrinking in importance. As previously mentioned, many administration jobs have now been automated. Fewer people working on routine tasks reduces the need for supervisors. Jobs in advertising media have radically changed now that newspapers and magazines are in decline. The job of family medical doctor has given way to specialists and assistants.

But new jobs have arisen to take their place, and some old ones have increased in demand. Here are some titles that have been discussed in the news recently.

| | | |
|---|---|---|
| Arborist | Heating and Cooling Installer | Program Evaluator |
| Cognitive Behavioral Therapist | Higher Education Administrator | Risk Manager |
| Curriculum Designer | Immigration Expert | Science Researcher |
| Cybercrime Investigator | Information Architect | Search Engine Optimizer |
| Data Miner | Interactive Creative Director | Security Planner |
| Diagnostic Imager | Knowledge Management | Small Farmer |
| Environmental Educator | Medical Researcher | Social Media Marketer |
| Environmental Engineer | Network Engineer | User Experience Designer |
| Genetic Counselor | Neuro Physicist | Video Game Designer |
| Health Informatics | Occupational Therapist | Web Content Manager |
| Healthcare Case Manager | Optometrist | |
| Healthcare Practice Manager | Patient Advocate | |

## GOOGLE COMPETENCIES

The Internet is a powerful tool that can help you to expand your narrow perceptions. You can connect your current competencies to unimagined activities in the workplace using search engines such as Google.

Entering competencies into Google brings the following ideas about the kind of work roles in which competencies can be utilized. You will get information from professional associations, conference agendas, consulting services, educational offerings, product and service descriptions, company PR releases, related articles in the media, and job descriptions.

Enter your competency, a question, or an area of interest into the search box of Google. The spaces separating the words act like the Boolean operator 'AND' and will return documents on which all of the words occur. The more words you enter, the more focused your search becomes. If you want to expand your search, enter 'OR' between the words and you will see documents which also contain the words individually. All letters are treated as lower case, so it does not matter whether you capitalize. Google ranks returns based on the number of sites that are linked to it. Those with many links are assumed to have a better reputation and so are more likely to provide a valuable information, and so they are returned first. The number of times a word appears on a page and its placement on the page also determine the order of returned pages. A powerful way of narrowing and focusing is to place a '+' before a word to require that it is on a returned page, or a '-' to require that it not be on a returned page.

Every Google results page has on the left sidebar a downward facing arrow and the phrase, 'Show search tools.' Clicking on this shows that you can filter your results by time frame, social connectedness, location, visited frequency, shopping opportunities, and relatedness.

Question yourself. Would you have known about all of these options for using your competencies?

Competency: communicating tactfully to coordinate events

Roles: communications planner for international development, production coordinator for advertising

Competency: putting multiple variables into a sequence

Roles: using arrays in computer programming, understanding global politics

Competency: deciding the best strategy to achieve a goal

Roles: consulting to improve productivity, strategizing for health care reform

Competency: organizing concepts in new ways

Roles: organizing business knowledge, recommending new ways to achieve customer value

Competency: inspiring people with new ideas

Roles: developing new ventures as an economist, promoting sustainable development

## BUZZ WORDS AND PHRASES

The majority of meaning on the Internet is contained in words. Some words take on additional power because they are used by a large number of people to mean the same thing. They are called 'buzz' words because people are buzzing around them. Some of the words are well known program titles, such as the business quality improvement phrase 'Sigma Six' or the holistic healing phrase 'meditation based stress reduction.' Browsers feature automatic phrase completion, with the phrases shown below the text entry box as you enter words. They are often useful buzz words.

Searching for buzz words takes time, but the effort is worth it.

Entering 'public health planning' and doing some searching brings up 'accountability indicators' as a common phrase. Entering that brings up many new and useful sites.

Are you interested in supply chain management? You will find that 'RFID Applications in Retail' is a useful buzz phrase.

There is software available to doing most anything. If you are interested in investigating the entertainment field, you will see that 'animations' are hot. 'Animation software' is a big category.

If you are interested in education and enter 'charter schools', you will see a buzz around 'charter school funding.' Try entering 'charter school funding +foundation.'

Main street jobs, an occupational trend, has taken on buzz phrase status. It brings information about the Adams Moran festival, a forward looking economic development project.

To transform we need to organize data so that we see its meaning and translate it into action. The first step is to recognize the data clusters that are out there that are relevant to us. The next step is to create our own meaning by selecting our own organizing idea and gathering data elements around it. We then create our own knowledge map which provides a place for new data elements that we discover and which can be easily rearranged as new ideas emerge. It's important to realize that we can create this organizer ourselves, rather than using an organizer someone else has identified.

## COMPETENCY MODELS

Numerous studies have been made to identify what effective people do in designated occupations. It is mind expanding and reinforcing to see actions that you do well as part of these models. If you are considering an occupation, look for a competency model and see if it contains some actions you typically do well.

http://www.jobbehaviors.com/Candidate/Default.aspx

Over fifty behavior-based occupational selection exams will give you insight into how the actions you do well fit with what creates success in each occupation.

http://www.microsoft.com/education/competencies/default.mspx

Eight competency studies were done in occupations in education.

http://www.thinkingpattern.com/downloads/Project%20Management%20competencies.pdf

This sample report will give you an idea of some of the elements of effective project management.

http://hr.uth.tmc.edu/Training_Development/perplan/competencies.PDF

This provides an insight into customer service competencies.

http://www7.acs.ncsu.edu/hr/classcomp/cband/purchasing/purch-mgr.pdf

This outline will let you see how your actions compare to those of successful purchasing managers.

You can search additional models by entering an occupation name and then "competencies" into a search engine such as Google.

The first sign that you need to overcome limiting stereotypes and assumptions is that you think that this concern does not apply to you. A few of the many resources available in the Internet have been presented. Now, resolve to allocate a part of each week to breaking out of your limiting views.

- What limitations do you have regarding your career? Can you recall a discussion about careers where you gave a "yes, but" reply, as in "Yes, that might be possible but not for me"? What topic were you discussing?

- How are your stereotypes about careers hurting you?

- What do you hope is available in a career for you? How can you discover whether such an opportunity already exists? If it does not, how can you make it a reality?

## CHAPTER SEVEN

# INTERACTING THROUGH WALKING

In this mode, career and work seekers physically walk and drive around to contact people to learn about what is happening in the economy, see job announcements, apply for jobs, and get ideas about new career options.

Picture a vibrant business neighborhood with sandwich boards on the sidewalk, seeking customers for all kinds of professions such as acupuncture practitioners, investment consultants, lawyers. Just as you would notice the signs as you walked along, you need to notice what is happening in the world around you. Look beyond what the media feed you. See what businesses are starting in your area. Which businesses are adding employees and growing? What ones are they replacing? Recognize that organizations with fewer than fifteen employees employ most people. You can walk into a business of that size, whether a manufacturer, a software consulting firm, or an advertising agency, and talk to real people to learn what is happening, what opportunities are coming up.

Job opportunities in your neighborhood are increasing. Our economy is shifting from production and distribution methods that rely on low-cost energy to methods that rely on person-to-person relationships. People are trying to source their food from within a hundred-mile radius of where they live. In community-supported agriculture, farmers contract with people to deliver their fresh produce to them weekly. As individuals' preferences shift from getting in a car and driving to get what they need to looking to their neighbors as the source for goods and services, jobs that meet personal needs in specific vicinity will increase.

When you are walking around, keep in mind that all work involves meeting the needs of people in some way. What are the needs of the people you are seeing and how are they being met? Are their needs to have a better appearance, improved health, and more convenience being met? Ask yourself about the needs of the owners of businesses you are seeing. How they are being met now? Are they succeeding at running smooth operations, understanding their market, developing ideas, and selling the resulting products or services? What kind of help do they need, and are you flexible enough to do it?

One of my clients in dire need of a job picked a busy street and knocked on every door. He found a job as an apprentice in a funeral home. Another with management experience walked through a loading dock to meet people and ended up as warehouse manager. Another person knocked on the door of a game development company and became a programmer for them.

If you are going for a job that requires confidence in reaching out to new people, dropping in to say hello with tact can powerfully demonstrate that you have the ability to initiate difficult contacts. One person obtained a job in fund raising for a major university by walking in and engaging someone whose office door was open. The searcher showed that he had the culture and mannerisms to fit into a situation requiring social skills and the tact and courage to initiate relationships.

- In your city or town, picture a neighborhood in which you would like to walk. What do you see in your mental picture before visiting? Then visit. After you walk around, what additional observations did you make—about businesses, traffic, people on the sidewalks, advertising along the streets, etc.?

- What is something helpful that you have discovered by walking around in the past, either intentionally or unintentionally?

- Make a list of your own needs that are not being fulfilled in an optimal way. Are you interested in investigating how one of the related services can be improved?

## Chapter Eight

# Interacting Through Paper and Computer Screen

The most utilized job finding process uses words on paper or computer screens. Information about career opportunities and job announcements are found on Internet job sites, in magazines and newspapers, and on bulletin boards in companies. Individuals apply to the openings via entering their cover letter and résumé into the companies' candidate database by email and, occasionally, by land mail.

Recruiters post many of these ads so prepare yourself for the response you will likely get from them. On the plus side for this mode of work and career searching, you have something specific to reach out to, a published job opening. On the down side, you are putting out effort in a single direction along with hundreds of others, all but one of whom will not get the position. Some of the applicants will have contacts within the company, some may even have an "in" with a job that the company must publish publicly, and some will have the perfect fit. You, on the other hand, might be under- or overqualified. If you are only responding to published job opportunities in your search, you will quickly run out of emotional reserve because so much of your effort will fail to provide positive results.

Approximately 25 percent of jobs are filled in this way. The percentage is higher for technical jobs and professional jobs that are difficult to fill and lower for management jobs. This means that you could spend about 25 percent of your effort on this tactic, which would still allow the other methods to keep you emotionally on track. Or, if you are qualified for a job with high demand, such as in the technical area, you might decide to place a much greater emphasis on the published market. You would put your résumé into as many places as possible as well as respond to posted ads and initiate contact in places where you think a job might exist.

Most job seekers assume that what used to be the standard procedure for applying for work still pervades the job market. First, job seekers read about job openings and get instructions for applying. Then they email their letter of interest and résumé. Next, the applicant usually assumes the submitted material will go through a single review tier where one person reads it. In composing the letters and résumés, the applicant needs to make that assumption and also prepare for something else.

A person will not review the application materials submitted on paper or computer screens unless the preparer has made the submissions attractive to the actual first-tier reviewer—the automated search. Everything the applicant writes goes into a computer database. A human will never review it unless it successfully appeals to the data-mining algorithm.

Your materials may be placed in the database from your email. You may also be asked to create a résumé for the database or paste your résumé and letter of interest directly into their database. Or, you may place your résumé into an Internet career site database that is searched by subscribers for relevant résumés that are imported into their database. In any case, your résumé will be selected only if the system finds a match between the words in the job announcement and the words in your résumé. Words in certain locations, such as job titles, get more points. Words that are repeated get more points. Identify your important key words, and include them where possible in places such as your Profile, your competency paragraphs, your key word list, the bullets that describe your job responsibilities, and your accomplishment bullets.

People in the human resources (HR) department write many
of the job announcements, and they do not always keep the details
about positions updated. They do not always include everything that
is required for success on the job. That is the reason why you should
include in your application some of your priority competencies that
have not been specifically requested. Your application will have some
of your personality and will stand out, and the job opportunity you will
find will have some elements that are important to you.

## E-RÉSUMÉ FORMAT

The résumé that you paste into the database should be formatted to
be read in a text editor. You might not like how your résumé looks
because the formatting added by your word processing program, such
as Microsoft Word, might not be utilized. Use only formatting which
comes from your keyboard. Justify everything left. Use capitals for
emphasis rather than boldface. Use asterisks from the key board rather
than bulleted lists, and do not use italics. To begin your reformatting
from Word, save your document as "Text Only." Then reopen it in .txt
mode and make your adjustments.

## KEY WORD SUMMARY

Look at all of the functions you have performed in the past. Identify a
large number of phrases that are generally used to describe the skills
and knowledge you have used in performing these functions. These
are the phrases employers and recruiters will use in searching for the
people they want to speak with. The search engine doesn't care whether
upper or lower case is used, but capitalizing the first letter looks better.
Here are examples of some key words. You should be able to identify
about twenty key word phrases that apply to you. Put them at the top
of your résumé because some algorithms give words at the top of the
résumé higher importance.

Supply Chain Management, Program Management, Sigma Six, Team Building, Participative Management, Action Research, Balanced Scorecard, Consultant Selling

## *JOB APPLICATION INTEREST LETTERS*

A letter of interest provides specific examples of your doing what the job requires, and so it goes beyond your résumé and adds an important emphasis.

Read the ad carefully and create a letter that adds emphasis to your résumé based upon what the ad calls for. Many ads for jobs request the letter, and when they do, it becomes a very important part of your application. Even if one is not requested, you may decide that the potential benefit warrants your effort in writing one. It gives you more control over how the potential employer sees you, expanding upon the factual nature of your résumé. It summarizes the match between your qualifications and the company's requirements. It emphasizes your relevant interests, which adds punch to your application, and highlights an ability more specifically than your résumé does. Finally, it expresses interest in having a subsequent contact.

Your letter will have paragraphs about your interests and abilities. Examples and specific information can increase the effectiveness of both sections. But make sure they relate to the job you are seeking. As you write applications and make the effort to think of examples, many more will come to mind. The longer you work at this, the better you will become, identifying more relevant examples as you go along. In fact, writing interest letters is an effective way of building work and career searching ability.

Put the interest paragraph first. Employers value it, you will stand out, and they will remember you. They know that an applicant whose interests closely match those needed for the job will be a good fit with the company, make a better employee, and be easier to manage. Your interests are most memorable and appealing part of you.

In your letters, maximize impact by clearly stating an idea and then following it with a relevant example. You give the reader one idea to consider, and then effectively expand upon it with an example, which brings a picture to mind. And people remember pictures better than mere words.

A good letter, such as this one responding to an opening for a product manager, contains the following elements.

State that you match the company's primary requirements. Do this in the introductory paragraph, and be specific about why you are making that statement.

> "Your announcement for a Product Manager stresses your desire for a person with proven entrepreneurial successes. In my most recent position, I used original marketing ideas to increase market share steadily over the past three years. In addition, I have the media planning and teamwork experiences you are seeking."

Present specific applicable interests. The company wants to know that you are strongly interested in working in the position it is advertising.

> "One of my primary interests is to understand the profile of the people who purchase the products I am managing. For example, I directed the design of a survey by consulting with a psychologist and testing trial versions. We surveyed a sample of 100 customers and used the resulting profile information to design more effective advertising."

Present specific applicable abilities. You should present examples that contain more specific detail than what you have put on your résumé.

> "One of my additional abilities is to manage projects. For one, I considered all of the developers and support people as part of the team. One of the reasons for our success was that I personally solicited every person's ideas and insured that they were considered in the meetings we had."

Expand your background and move the reader's eyes to your résumé. The reviewer is probably reading your letter and glancing at the highlights of your résumé. So, make the connection clear, and point out the part of the résumé you want the reviewer to notice.

> "As you can see from my résumé, I have held a series of positions with increasing responsibility that lead perfectly to the position of Product Manager at your company."

Close. Show your positive expectation.

> "Thank you for reviewing my qualifications. I am looking forward to learning more about your exciting opportunity."

Present enough about your interests and abilities so that you complete about a page and a half. That length is the best proof that you are truly interested.

The best strategy for finding your ideal position is to resolve to use the published job market to your advantage. Apply to a set number of jobs in the most efficient way possible. In this way, you will need to stretch your view of what you are qualified to do, which helps push you out of limited thinking and increases the possibilities available to you.

## CHAPTER NINE

# INTERACTING IN CONVERSATIONS

"When it comes to getting a job, it's who you know that counts!" Frustrated job seekers often make this exclamation, and it's true, but not for the reason most people think. Managers rarely hire their friends. They know they cannot confront a friend as they would an employee. In addition, all managers would be deeply discredited and embarrassed if their newly hired friend did not work out. They rarely take the risk.

One of the biggest reasons a person succeeds in work searching and a career has to do with the people he or she knows—but not because he or she was hired by those people. Instead, who the person knows through social networking leads to job possibilities.

Managers do hire people they meet in the course of doing business or through a referral from a business or social connection. And they do listen to what their connections tell them about people. Everyone can meet enough people so that they succeed in being referred. Jobs are found through interacting and conversing with people approximately 75 percent of the time.

Most people who are between jobs begin their job search through the written mode. They work on their résumé, search published jobs, and make applications. If they want to insure they are taking the best possible steps, they might contact a career counselor.

One of the important goals of career counselors in their initial meeting with clients is to bring out and reinforce their history of initiating and maintaining relationships. This might include relating to someone with a similar interest at a social event or participation in professional activities. They might also bring out connection possibilities such as past workmates and schoolmates, connections on a team, fellow volunteers on a community group, and consultants working together. The positive feeling of having those connections will outweigh the understandable negative feeling of being out of work and isolated. Job seekers who can place uppermost in their awareness a history of positive social connections can counteract the understandable hesitance of initiating contacts when they are looking for work. Networking in searching for a career and work can be just as much fun and just as successful as those past contacts.

Most people find a way to engage in this kind of interacting with people which suits their personality. You can confirm this by asking people you know how they have obtained their past jobs. You will be surprised by how many found out about an opportunity or got an advantage in the selection process as a result of a personal contact.

The path to a new job involves meeting other people often in arranged situations but sometimes in low-key settings and everyday encounters. You can make even meetings with strangers enjoyable with the right attitude—staying relaxed and knowing others want to help you. Here are how some clients in career counseling created connections that led to work.

- *A banking manager new in town talked with a neighbor who worked at a bank that was looking for someone similar.*

- *A customer service manager discovered through networking that he had an experience advantage for a city job he otherwise would not have applied for.*

- *A finance person found out the details of a job through networking, and this enabled him to be selected for it.*

- *A recently discharged military officer took a real estate appraisal class and was hired by the teacher.*

- *An administrator visited a former workmate working in another company, and discovered a job opening she obtained in that company.*

- *A financial analyst got a job in educational administration after talking with a person in a community school who was receptive to talking with their public.*

- *A manager with recycling experience approached a fellow Little League parent working in the same industry and got a job at his company.*

- *A software developer met a new colleague at a church job group. with whom he started a business.*

- *A bank analyst with marketing abilities and no experience outside of banking networked into a non-profit and became its development executive.*

- *A HR trainer became a compensation analyst thanks to a referral from a neighbor.*

- *An entrepreneur networking to build attendance at a community event was hired by a person he was selling to.*

A discussion with an executive or technical recruiter is an example of personal contact. Although many are willing to talk with people who are between jobs, they rarely find positions for them. The reason why companies pay them handsomely is that recruiters find an individual who brings something special, such as ideas from a competitor, to the client. Most job changes that occur through recruiters result from their initiating contact with a person who is already working. Often the person they place was not even contemplating a change. Talking with a staffing company recruiter, who primarily places non-management personnel, can be an effective personal connection for some occupations. Many companies use them to cover temporary needs. Also, many companies use them as a source of new employees through "Temp to Hire" contracts.

Conversing with people to find work is done one contact at a time. The process begins with talking with a current contact, Contact #1, who refers you to someone new who knows what is happening in a segment of the job market that fits you, Contact #2. That person uses his or her specific knowledge to refer you to another person, Contact #3, who has or knows of a job opening immediately or sometime in the future. You have found success through a link of three. Three links have been shown in sociological studies to be the most common way people find opportunity. Everyone can identify a current connection and reach out to begin the process.

## PREPARING FOR NETWORKING

Networking is an extremely powerful career transition tool. When people make a dramatic move, the primary reason for their strong direction comes from an interaction with one or more others who changed their perceptions. You may have experienced the power of words from another in a different setting. Think of a time when you were walking in a beautiful place, thinking that you were enjoying it as much as possible. Then you met someone who brought your attention to a specific aspect of the scene, maybe made a comment on the bright colors of the flowers. Did that interaction have the effect of intensifying your enjoyment of the flowers as you continued your walk? Similarly, in career networking, what others say can have an extremely powerful impact on our experience.

Because networking is so important, a special effort should be made to prepare for a networking session. Ask yourself these questions:

**What are my real feelings about networking?** Many people read about the importance of networking and pay attention to the topic in career transition workshops but really have no intention of doing it. They may feel they have invested in their career in other ways, such as education and experiences with leading employers, and want a return on that investment versus having to learn a new skill called networking. They survived after a long search for a job that matched their past labels. But that's not possible today. Because the old jobs do not exist, you need to resolve to become adept at networking.

**How easy is it for my personality type to engage in networking?** If you know in advance that rather than approaching new people with excitement about a new relationship and ideas for inspiring career directions, fear will set in, you can prepare. If anxiety is an obstacle, use the techniques in Chapter 13 to deal with it.

**Do you feel that you are equal to the other person in professional stature and accomplishment?** It's important to realize that the other person enjoys talking with colleagues and hopes to broaden his or her own thinking by talking with you. Your contact probably knows about lots of opportunities, but they are below his or her conscious awareness. They will be brought to the surface more easily if there is a feeling of mutuality and rapport. Picture and feel yourself interacting in a relationship among equals.

**Are you ready to listen?** Many people have as an unrecognized priority a desire to talk about their own career. Your contact will enjoy it more if you listen. You will learn more if you listen. Yet, many networkers do not listen enough. Plan to change this tendency with your feet. As you walk from your car to the front door for the meeting, every time your left foot hits the ground, say to yourself, "Listen!"

**What is the other person interested in?** Sources of information might be their LinkedIn profile, a Web site of a current or former business, an article they wrote, or their comment on a blog. Go to the Web site of the person's current company. You might learn some background information that changes the questions you ask and the leading statements you make. At the least, your research will yield information that will improve your rapport building at the beginning of the session.

**What does the person know that can help you?** Brainstorm with yourself prior to your meeting to improve your ability to brainstorm in the meeting. Make a list. Think about some "what if's." Ask yourself—

What if they are planning to launch a new product? What might it be?

What if they want to make things more efficient? How would that work?

What if they are going to expand their business? In what direction would they go?

**Which of your competencies will be viewed as most valuable by the other person?** If you are talking with a person with special knowledge, you need to bring out the part of you that will lead to a feeling of commonality. If the person is involved in technology, you might be able to say something about automation. If the person is in health care, you could talk about the politic of health reform. Etc.

There are three kinds of networking conversations that coincide with stages of a work search. It's important that both you and your networking partner have the same understanding of the stage you are in and the purpose of your conversation. The first stage is networking for discovering new options. You the networker are presenting your accomplishments which can be used in a number of ways. Your contact needs to understand that you are not detailing your assets for a specific occupation. The second stage is networking to build a niche. Your purpose is to build credibility in a specific occupation. Your partner needs to have experiences in it and become an information and referral source for you. This is not the time for a wide ranging discussion of many possibilities. The third stage is networking to market yourself as a consultant. Here it's important to not be seen as merely looking for ideas and relationships. You need to convey that you have moved away from exploring and developing. You are the competent performer others need, now!

The following sections will help you to go through the stages of a search: exploring, niche building, and marketing. You will learn to say the right thing about yourself at the right time and to ask questions that will lead to fruitful discussions. But you need to be opportunistic and flexible. When you are in an exploring conversation and notice that your networking contact is interested in providing information about a specific occupation, you need to change your stage and ask some questions about a niche. You might have the opportunity to jump to the third stage and ask if a proposal is appropriate and be ready to go for it

# NETWORKING FOR DISCOVERING NEW OPTIONS

Humans instinctively connect with others, and networking plays upon this natural tendency. But when asking for help with something as sensitive as one's career, complications can set in. The exploratory networking steps suggested here are the best way to proceed. They work far more effectively and engage the two parties more strongly than the oft-touted informational interview. That method is a one-way process in which the networking source presents what he or she does, and the networker merely listens. Without two-way communication—a give and take of information, of desires, of experiences and insights—the source has no certainty about how you will use the information for your career progress and so is less interested in interacting, brainstorming, and describing possibilities.

The steps suggested here do not involve asking for help with your career decisions. The networker needs to project that he or she is quite able to manage his or her career and make great decisions. Nor is the networker looking for a job opening. That approach results in a dead end because most people do not have that information. Instead, the networker is asking questions and making leading statements that result in a brainstorming session that combines information in a way that raises new job options for the networker.

Networking for discovering new options brings people together and creates something valuable. When done right, it leads to meaningful work and enriches a person's life in many ways. Successful networkers do the following:

- Begin talking with people they already know and get referrals based on their unique competencies.

- Conduct interviews that are enjoyable brainstorming sessions that benefit both participants. From the new insights created, both people feel they have some good ideas that they can use to be more successful.

- Let the other person feel he or she is helping because people usually enjoy helping.

- Keep in touch with those in the best position to help. Over time, their sources hear about an opportunity and relay the information back to the networker.

- Meet people in hiring companies who can push their résumé to the top of the pile of candidates for a job opening.

- Position themselves so managers see them as filling a need in the company. The manager creates a job, and the networkers have an advantage because they have planted a seed that they are talented and capable.

- Talk positively about themselves, presenting themselves as upbeat and optimistic, and thus increase their success in subsequent activities.

- Listen and make an effort to expand their perceptions. Information heard from another person provides a powerful way to broaden perspectives and change behavior for the better.

Even with these benefits, most people shy away from reaching out and meeting new people in a way that will help their job search. But for every reason they cite to avoid networking, we can cite at least one better reason to jump in and start networking. Some people are embarrassed to be between jobs, even at a time when career transitions from major companies are extremely commonplace. Some do not want to intrude on another person's life, even though successful people recognize the value of expanding their perceptions by talking with people, and even though networking effectiveness can be learned by everyone. Some may feel uncomfortable approaching someone they do not know, even though it might not be as uncomfortable as being without a job.

## RÉSUMÉ FOR DISCOVERING OPTIONS

A résumé for exploring encourages your reader to see you first as a person with usable competencies and second as a person with a certain job history. When people look at your résumé, they immediately form an impression. If your readers see your job titles and past employers first, they may put you into those boxes. Your goal is to break out of what your past job titles say about you. Help others to think of you in a broader way by beginning your résumé with your priority competencies. These set the stage for an expanded discussion about where you can utilize the abilities you enjoy most and do best. If you have effectively presented your competencies, you will see that they can be combined in unimagined ways to fit into existing jobs and jobs that will be created.

Therefore, a résumé that begins with competency paragraphs is recommended for the options discovery stage of a search. Jenny used the results from her prioritization grid as the starting point. She placed her priority competencies at the top, grouped other competencies, and changed some of the words to match what she knew was popular in the job market. On her résumé, which follows, the headings are bolded. Each heading is followed by supporting evidence, consisting of a description of experience or a specific example. When contacts read the rest of this résumé, they will look for evidence about these competencies. They will see her as a person with competencies that can be used in many ways. They will see her more broadly than if the first thing they see is job titles. They are more likely to suggest interesting ways that your combination of competencies can be utilized from their point of view. Notice that the Interests/Activities section provides additional supporting experiences. Minor employment experiences do not have to be listed.

---

**Exploring Résumé**

Jenny Reed
20180 Success Way, Redmond, WA 98052, jreed@att.net, 425-123-4567

**Persuasive Speaking and Advocacy.** Effectively discussed issues in many classroom situations. Improved the performance of a sales team by speaking at meetings and by example.

**Cultural Understanding.** Changed my approach to others based on an expanded understanding of their culture, improving the relationship of our department to the others. Traveled extensively, developed an understanding of other cultures, and interacted successfully with people I met.

**Creative Thinking.** Created a chart that compared options for automating the workflow of our department. The new system I helped to develop improved the accuracy of time and budget tracking for complicated purchases.

**Teaching/Empathy.** Engaged clients as massage practitioner by conveying an understanding of their situation; taught and carried out healing techniques in a caring way.

### Work Experience

**Massage Practitioner,** Self-employed, Seattle, WA 2005–present

- Developed a marketing program and sold services to make the practice a success.
- Provided long-term healing and formed lasting relationships with clients.

**Research Program Coordinator,** University of Washington, Seattle, WA 1998–2003

- Oversaw design and implementation procedures for data management.
- Built strong relationships with the team, which improved communication and efficiency.

**Sales Representative,** Southwestern Publishing, Seattle, WA 1995–1997

- Worked long hours to make contacts and close sales.
- Formed ongoing and productive relationships with customers.

### Education

**AA Humanities,** Shoreline Community College, Shoreline, WA

### Interests/Activities

Travel. Spent 6 months in China understanding the culture and learning healing methods.

Personnel Development. Study methods to help people improve their lives.

This résumé effectively summarizes who she is now in her career, and where she wants to go. She can use it to introduce herself to others in her networking approach letters and to leave behind as a reminder for other kinds of meetings. And, it provides a handy reminder about the most productive things she can say about herself.

## THIRTY-SECOND COMMERCIAL

Active career and work seekers are challenged to present themselves verbally as they get involved in meeting people, for example, when riding an elevator, which on the average lasts thirty seconds. Other examples are at professional association meetings, conferences, and non-work social occasions. Put yourself in other people's shoes; ask what they are interested in knowing about you. They want to know your background, what you are interested in doing now, and how they can help. To convey what you want to do now, it's to your advantage to identify the competencies you want to use rather than a job title. Most people will have ideas for how your competencies might be used, but they may not know of a job opening for a job title. Here is a thirty-second commercial for Jenny, tailored specifically for discovering options while networking.

> "I have work experience in selling, program coordination, and direct helping in a health care setting. I am especially interested in carrying forward my successes in persuasive speaking, cultural understanding, and creative thinking. For example, I motivated a sales team by expressing strong advocacy for our product and tailoring my speech specifically to the characteristics of the group. I used my creativity in improving research processes. I am looking for people who can help me identify career options that take advantage of these talents."

## NETWORKING IN YOUR CURRENT COMPANY

All companies want their employees fully engaged in creating great products or services and taking good care of their customers. They want them to make a dedicated effort to think of ways to be even more effective. And they want them committed to having a long-term career with them. That is why management discusses possible future jobs in the company as part of its performance review and why managers react favorably when one of their employees initiates a career discussion.

Even you can have an expanding future in your company! If you have just started out, you may not think so because you may feel overwhelmed by being asked to do tasks you never imagined, including some you do not like. But look around at someone who is successful in your current company and notice all of the extra things they are doing. If you have worked in the company for many years, you may think you have lost all opportunities for advancement or a positive change because you have made suggestions in the past that have been ignored. But with the self-analysis and methods presented in this book, you can present yourself again, this time more effectively. Look at your priority competencies and apply them to one of your company's products or services. Ask yourself what improvements you would make to them and what steps you would take to bring them about.

Some companies have a formal mentor program in which senior people make themselves available to offer guidance and help to younger employees. No such program in your company? See that as an opportunity! Show yourself as a motivated employee and make a positive change by reaching out to form a mentor relationship—you and another whose effectiveness, attitude, performance, etc. you wish to emulate. Initiate a discussion based on a common interest other than a job. Then, move on to suggesting another session to brainstorm career possibilities.

*Elizabeth, a savvy and successful work finder, described the process she used to obtain a prized job in her company as "romancing." She took these steps in moving to a better job:*

- *Bonded with people by getting them to talk, showing an interest in what they were saying, listening intently, and responding to their comments.*

- *Reinforced what the other person said and showed how it could be utilized to solve one of their pressing problems.*

- *Told competency stories about herself that applied to a problem the other person was working on.*

- *Showed her strong interest by making an effort to find out about and contribute interesting ideas that could help the other person.*

Now picture yourself doing this on your current job. Who could you talk with? Start with your current manager. As momentum builds, ask him or her to ask a manager in another department that interests you for permission to talk with one of his or her lead employees, such as the one on page 142 and 145. Have the discussions before work, during lunch, or after work, and keep them short.

Any interpersonal interaction with someone new involves moving out of your comfort zone. Everyone feels fear and anxiety; that's normal. Specific ways to combat these feelings are presented in the section Overcoming Obstacles. One way which will help is to plan to make your interaction an easy-going, enjoyable brainstorming session. When two people meet and exchange possibilities, new insights are generated, creating a positive feeling.

## HELPFUL ATTITUDES

**Be humble, be helped.** In many business cultures, an unwritten rule says that you won't get anything of value unless you offer something of equal value. Many other segments of society support this idea. For instance, most LinkedIn users put on their profile page that they are looking for networking contacts and business opportunities. No one says that he or she is looking for free knowledge and contacts. But that is exactly the correct approach to take. You may well provide equal value for the information you seek—ideas about opportunities from the other person's experience, inside information about what works in those environments, referrals if possible—but you don't know for sure. So humbly ask for help. You will discover that others will greatly enjoy helping you, especially when you present this request honestly. And the more quickly you overcome embarrassment and reach out for help, the sooner you will learn this valuable lesson: people feel good helping others, they welcome the chance to help, and your request for help makes it all possible.

**Adopt an open-minded brainstorming attitude.** Brainstorming involves inspiring ideas in the other person that apply to you. And that basic concept requires you to keep an open mind, to welcome input from the other, and to avoid squelching anything put forth. Even the silliest of ideas can lead to a solid platform for action. In the best scenario, both people learn interesting things and have fun in the exchange, you get a new point of view on yourself and the world, and the other person feels good about helping you. Everyone wins.

**Initially follow and then prepare to lead.** Your primary goal centers on building a relationship, and this requires a readiness to adopt the other person's agenda before trying tactfully to turn it towards a direction that you think will produce results you want. Others may not have an agenda, and you will need to provide all of the leadership during the session.

**Keep the agenda brief and simple.** Plan for a brief discussion in which the other person does most of the talking about what he or she knows is happening in your areas of interest.

**Overcome the temptation to talk too much and prepare to listen and take notes.** Many times, a networking interview provides the first opportunity in a long time for a work seeker to talk about his or her career. Do not give in! Avoid the urge to talk too much about yourself, and instead, adopt a listening attitude. Talking about your self is exhilarating until you sit down after the session to review your notes for information that will help you, only to find ... nothing. Learn by listening.

## SET UP THE MEETING

Before you meet with someone for your brainstorming session, you need to let him or her know your intent and request a time for the meeting. Even if you know a person well and a meeting is assured, a Networking Approach Letter has several advantages over a phone-only contact. Presenting your emotional maturity and setting expectations is crucial at this point, and if you depend on a phone call, you may gloss over some of these steps, and your meeting might not be as effective. Another benefit is that, if you take the time to write a letter, you are showing your motivation and implying that you will take the time to prepare for the meeting so that it has a positive outcome.

Your communication can be via land letter or email. A letter will have much more impact because it will not compete with hundreds of other messages, and it shows that you are making an effort in your networking project. Although an email is more convenient, I recommend that you make it a practice to use letters.

No one likes to be spammed, which occurs when people send out repeated blanket emails to everyone, doing nothing but clogging up their email inbox. Nor do most people want to annoy others by spamming. But people naturally hesitate to approach individuals, even with legitimate requests, out of respect for their privacy. If you feel this about someone, should you honor that as a valid message to obey, or does it indicate an unfounded fear on your part? Can you learn to distinguish between the two and approach people in a tactful and appropriate way?

Using a letter or email to approach a networking prospect maximizes your chances of success in obtaining an in-person meeting. Your approach message conveys a number of important elements.

Rather than starting with your highest potential contact, begin your outreach with someone with whom you are comfortable for practice.

## START WITH A FRIEND

**Remind and reinforce mutual interests**. Refer to the past activities you worked on together, and reinforce your mutual interest that was shown.

The phrasing of this paragraph depends upon the kind of person you are approaching and where your commonality lies.

Common business experience:

> "We met at a conference on branding and talked about our products. I especially remember your insights about the need for more specificity in branding."

Neighbor:

> "As neighbors, we have talked about everything under the sun, from our children to vacations to home repairs. You may have heard that I am now in a career transition. Would it be possible to get together for some brainstorming to help broaden my perceptions about career possibilities related to some of the experiences you have had?"

Former work mate:

> "When we worked together at Smith Manufacturing, you always had good ideas about how to be more effective. Would it be possible for me to take advantage of your insights in brainstorming about where opportunities will be in our industry?"

**Be clear about your situation and expectations**. You are probably seeking ideas about a future direction and also information about actual opportunities.

> "You know that things have been in flux at work, and now I am in a career transition situation. I have identified the key competencies I want to carry forward, and I am talking with people such as you about where I can apply them."

**Request a brief meeting and emphasize a disclaimer**. Ask for a time in a way that demonstrates your flexibility, and make an extra effort to insure that the person knows you don't expect him or her to know of a job opening. This takes the pressure off. People want to help, but they do not want requests that they have no power to fulfill.

"Would it be possible to talk either by phone or in person for twenty minutes or so? You have a number of interesting experiences in the field I am exploring, and your perspective would be very helpful. I don't expect you to know of anything specific."

**Link to background information.** This provides an opportunity for the person to learn more about you to get some ideas ahead of time.

"You can see from my résumé, which follows, that I have successfully initiated and maintained contact with key people in distribution and retail situations through a variety of jobs."

**Express thanks and identify next steps.** You need to assume that you will have to initiate a phone contact. Set it up in your approach letter.

"Thanks for your time and effort on my behalf. I will call your office at the beginning of the week to identify the best time to meet."

### Networking Approach Email

Jim Roberts
Advertising Innovations

Hi Jim,

In the years we have known each other, your fresh ideas on a wide variety of topics have always impressed me, and I would appreciate your opinion and insight on my current situation.

You know that things have been in flux at work, and now I am beginning a career transition. I have identified my key areas of experience I want to carry forward, and I am talking with people such as you about where I can apply them.

Would it be possible to talk either by phone or in person for twenty minutes or so? Given your background and interesting experiences, your perspective would help me tremendously. I am not expecting you to know of anything specific.

You can see from my résumé, which follows, that I have successfully initiated and maintained contact with key people in distribution and retail situations.

Thanks for your time and effort on my behalf. I will call your office at the beginning of the week to identify the best time to meet.

Best regards.
Paul Smith
500 Totem Ave.
Kirkland, WA 98034
425-862-3794
psmith@yahoo.com

Résumé follows and is attached.

### APPROACHING SOMEONE NEW

You will use many of the same elements in this case as you would in the letter to someone you know. Be clear about your situation and expectations, request a brief meeting, link to background information, express thanks, and identify next steps. But your opening paragraph will have to address why you are contacting this person. Use a referral if you have one. Having a mutual acquaintance means that you two probably have more in common than just the friend. Ask your friend for some information about the person and play upon that in your letter. Citing your commonalities will increase the odds of having a valuable exchange of information.

**Start with the referral source if you have one.** If possible, be specific about what motivated your friend's referral.

"Frank Smith suggested that I contact you because of my interests and experiences in integrating human and technical processes."

**Expand upon the linking interest.** The other person wants to see positive results from the meeting by having an interesting discussion and providing some real help to you. You can intensify his or her motivation by mentioning the benefits you want to gain.

"From what he said, we both realize the importance of paying attention to the human interface issues of the many technical applications we are seeing today. Many have said that this holds one of the keys for increasing productivity and reducing stress on the job."

**Make a request and include a disclaimer.** This will show that you have prepared an agenda and intend to make this a beneficial exchange.

"Would it be possible to talk with you about some of the opportunities around this idea? At this time, I am exploring needs and opportunities to put my interests to work. You have experiences that will be very helpful to me in this endeavor, regardless of whether you know of anything specific."

**Present your related background and move eyes to your résumé.**
This will provide an overview to stimulate thinking prior to your meeting.

> "As you can see from my résumé, I have experiences developing
> software and managing IT projects. More recently, I have
> led efforts in human engineering."

**Make an action close.** Because you do not know this person
and a mutual friend referred you, assume your contact will appreciate
a phone call from you.

> "Thank you for considering a discussion. I will call in a few
> days to ask if a brief meeting will be possible."

### Networking Approach Letter

**Paul Boynton**
9 Elm Avenue, Seattle, WA 98115,
psmith@yahoo.com, 206-415-8645

October 20, 2008

Jim Green
Synergy Company
39 Anderson Blvd.
Bellevue, WA 98004

Dear Jim,

Frank Smith suggested that I contact you because of my interests and experiences in integrating human and technical processes. From what he said, we both realize the importance of paying attention to the human interface issues of the many technical applications we are seeing today. Many have said that this holds one of the keys for increasing productivity and reducing stress on the job.

Would it be possible to talk with you about some of the opportunities around this idea? At this time I am exploring needs and opportunities to put my interests to work. You have experiences which will be very helpful to me in this endeavor, regardless of whether you know of anything specific.

As you can see from my résumé, I have experiences developing software and managing IT projects. More recently, I have led efforts in human engineering.

Thank you for considering a discussion. I will call in a few days to ask if a brief meeting will be possible.

Best regards,

Paul Boynton

## *Successful Meetings*

The key to making your next job a step towards your meaningful work is meeting with, forming positive relationships with, and then keeping in touch with people who have ideas about how your competencies can be used.

In one of my most enjoyable and productive networking meetings, I had only one goal: to listen and bring out the person's interest and build on that. My expressing enthusiastic and genuine concern in his message and voicing my appreciation for what he was doing brought out a more lively tone in his voice. My summarizing his ideas caused him to dig more deeply into what he really thought, and he talked about managing employees in a way that would build a participative culture in a company. He then wanted me to speak, and my description about a project for increasing employee interest in their careers fit right in to what he had discussed. I easily worked in an idea for an employee engagement workshop, and it clicked because he saw that we had something in common. Now, we are communicating every couple of weeks about mutual progress on our ideas, and I know that if he comes across something that will help in finding my work he will let me know.

Here are some elements that need to be included in your interactions to make them most effective.

**Connect and set expectations.** State appreciation for the connection you are having and remind the other person that you aren't counting on him or her to solve your problem of finding a job.

> "Thanks for meeting with me. First of all, I would like to emphasize that my primary goal is not to learn about a job from you but to gather information for my job search."

**Make a strong statement about yourself.** Go beyond your past job titles. Present three of your competencies that convey your priority interests and abilities up-front. You want to give the other person crucial information for helping you. In this example, the person would add two more competencies to the statements about this one.

"Could I begin with a summary? I have a strong interest in helping people to see the positives rather than the negatives when it comes to change. For example, I recognize that people are defensive when a consultant comes in from the outside, and I have put people at ease through my firm attitude of openness."

**Use open-ended questions that elicit talk.** The goal is an enjoyable, easy-going brainstorming kind of interview.

"What kinds of places need this?"

(Your networking source states an idea)

"I've never thought of it in that way, but I'm interested in the idea. Tell me more."

**Ask for referrals when appropriate.** The best time to get a referral is when a person is relaxed, tuned in to you and the discussion, and thinking of something specific that interests you.

"That sounds especially interesting. Who can I talk to about that?"

**Pick up on and extend what the other person says.** Show your flexibility in fitting into new situations and enhancing what the other person says.

"Using collaboration technology in that way can also be a marketing tool. I have seen instances of that in my most recent work."

**End the conversation early and on an upbeat note, suggest keeping in touch, and always express gratitude.** It's more important to feel welcomed to return for further discussion than get all the possible information in one, uncomfortably prolonged conversation.

"You've helped me learn more about the field that most interests me and given me ideas about how to proceed. Thank you for your time and your insights. Could we keep in touch?"

It's common to find opportunity that will lead to a job offer during this initial networking stage. Using this guide for exploring possibilities, work seekers project less pressure for a job. They come across as relaxed and abundant. And in the sharing of ideas with the other, they demonstrate their own willingness to help. All of these positives often lead to a job.

## THANK-YOU MESSAGE

Sending a thank-you in a timely way will put a ribbon around your interaction. Writing the message the next day shows your appreciation more than anything else. And you get another benefit: Nothing puts you in a good frame of mind as powerfully as an expression of gratitude, here in the form of a thank-you note.

**Express thanks and appreciation.** Don't think that business interactions preclude expressions of positive emotions. Professionals do smile, even laugh once in a while! And they all appreciate genuine statements of gratitude.

"Thanks for the enjoyable and informative meeting. I appreciated your innovative thinking."

**Acknowledge and summarize what you learned**. You cannot say too often that the other person had good ideas. Cite at least one specific example to give credence to your thanks.

"You pointed out that everyone is figuring out how their employees can use social networking to achieve business goals, a valuable insight."

**Identify future actions.** This shows that the person did not waste his or her time with you, that the discussion will generate positive action on your part.

"I am looking forward to exploring the option of community development with the city."

**Suggest keeping in touch.** Your contact will be an antenna of opportunity for you, and so make it easy to stay in touch.

"I would appreciate being able to keep in contact."

Interacting with new people, drawing out their interests, matching with stories of your related successes, and primarily listening will lead you to meaningful work. How long should you carry out these kinds of career exploring and relationship building activities? All of the time. Continue to talk to people about new options as you zero in on a niche. This is one of the most successful ways for a person to find a new job that leads to fulfillment.

- How does this kind of interacting compare to what you are doing in your career advancement or job search activities now?

- What is an example of when you listened to another person and discovered something new?

- Does this kind of interacting come naturally to you, and if not, do you think you can learn it?

## EVALUATING OPTIONS

In the first month of a career transition, you might spend time catching up on some recreation, understanding your competencies and other assets, writing your résumé, and practicing interviewing. Then you should plan to spend at least two months in the exploring stage of your search. After that, you might begin exploring an option in depth. But which option? To insure that you don't waste your time heading down the wrong path, make a formal comparison of options. Even if you think you know which option is best, a formal comparison will increase your self-understanding and motivation.

### Jenny's Networking

*After two months of exploring written resources, Jenny talked with some people at her work who were easily accessible through her job. Talking with me about her feelings about her current career situation prior to her first meeting helped to put her in a listening frame of mind. But, once in the meetings, although the people wanted to help, the conversations didn't really flow. Afterwards, we identified some ways she could have acknowledged the other person more and some ways that the setting of the workplace was probably inhibiting. Next, she talked with a previous teacher who gave suggestions along professional lines. What helped her to see things in new ways was a meeting with a referral who was a sales person. Because sales people need to know what is happening in the world, they can provide valuable insights to the industry they cover. She was able to talk with a total of fifteen people, including workers in occupations and school admissions people.*

In their exploring, career and work finders see how they can combine their priority competencies with knowledge to be effective in an industry and often in a specific industry segment. Exploration brings out many occupation/industry possibilities, as well as information to compare the possibilities. The comparison factors would include desire to use certain abilities, desire to see certain kinds of results, preferring a certain work environment, schooling and time factors, financial realities, likelihood of success, match to current networks, and many more.

A decision-making grid, which follows, provides one way to evaluate the different options. It uses logic to assess the importance of each choice and assigns values to each so the best option stands out. You list the factors used in making the decision on the left. In the next column, give the number that shows weight or relative the importance of each factor. Each of the next columns contains one of the options you are considering. Here is an example of how to construct and use the grid.

### Jenny's Options Comparison

*Jenny summarized the results of her exploring into the decision-making grid, which follows. First, she listed all of the decision factors in her life that being involved in an occupation would impact. These included the competencies she wanted to use, the type of environment in which she would work, her free time, etc. Next, she assigned a relative weight, or weighting number, from 1 (low) to 3 (high), to each factor, based upon how important she saw it. For instance, relationships with people matter strongly with Jenny, so she gave the highest value to her competency for supporting relationships and to a work environment that provided friendships through teamwork.*

*She had one column for each of the options she was considering pursuing—law, teaching anthropology, and nursing. Under each option and for each decision factor, she assigned a value from 1 to 5, depending upon how well that option satisfied the factor. For instance, Option #1, Law, only slightly let her use her competency for helping through teaching, so she gave it a value of 2 on her scale of 1 to 5. For the same competency, Option #3, Nursing, would use it much more, so she gave it a value of 5.*

*To figure the relative importance of each factor in each option, Jenny then multiplied the factor's relative weight times the value under each option. For instance, for her first listed competency, speaking to advocate, she had assigned a relative weight of 2. Multiplying that times the 5 for how well Option #1 satisfied that factor gives 10; doing the same for Option #3 gives 2 times 3, or 6. She put these numbers in parentheses in the following chart.*

*Finally, she added all of the numbers in parentheses for each option. The option with the highest total shows that law would best satisfy the factors she was considering.*

*In making these estimates, Jenny deepened her understanding of what was important to her, and she broadened her understanding of some important aspects of occupational possibilities.*

| Decision Factors | Relative Weight (1 – 3) | Option #1 (1 – 5)<br><br>Law | Option #2 (1 – 5)<br><br>College Anthropology Prof | Option #3 (1 – 5)<br><br>Nursing |
|---|---|---|---|---|
| Competency: Speaking to advocate | 2 | 5(10) | 4(8) | 3(6) |
| Competency: Creativity and new ideas | 1 | 4(4) | 5(5) | 2(2) |
| Competency: Supporting via relationships | 3 | 4(12) | 3(9) | 5(15) |
| Desired Results: Social justice | 2 | 5(10) | 2(4) | 1(3) |
| Supportive Lifestyle: Easy on the family | 2 | 3(6) | 5(10) | 2(4) |
| Work Environment: Flexible and creative / Friendships with team | 1<br>3 | 4(4)<br>1(3) | 5(5)<br>2(6) | 2(2)<br>3(9) |
| Risk: Risk is low | 2 | 2(4) | 1(2) | 5(10) |
| Total: | | 53 | 49 | 51 |

Create a grid similar to the one Jenny did. List on the left side all of the various factors affecting your decision. Phrase them in positive terms so that a higher relative weight reflects your greater desire for that factor. For example, say "risk is low" rather than "degree of risk" (unless, of course, you want high risk!). Assign a number from 1 (unimportant) to 3 (very important) to each factor, depending upon its relative importance to you. Across the top, list each of your viable options. Then in the boxes, give a numeric value, here 1 (low score) to 5 (high score), representing how that option scores on that factor. Next multiply that number by the relative importance number, giving a weighted number for each box. Finally, add all the weighted numbers in each column. The highest scoring option indicates your best choice, based upon the information you have provided.

The grid provides one system for evaluating your options. It indicates the choice that makes the most sense from the standpoint of decision-making factors and occupational characteristics that you can verbalize and quantify. But you also need to tune into other sources of information and see whether you get the same message. For instance, in Jenny's case, she could spend time observing the "best" occupation and gauge her gut feeling. She could talk to others in that field and see if she had considered all relevant factors. And she could take a walk in a favorite beautiful place, quiet her mind, and listen to her intuition.

## NETWORKING FOR NICHE-BUILDING

On your path to finding your work, you have increased your self-understanding, renewed acquaintances, met new people, identified possibilities, and evaluated options. Although you might continue your exploring activities, now you delve into one of your options in more depth. You will identify a niche that utilizes your strengths, feeds your interests, and builds upon the information you have gathered. But you will need to add more experiences and competencies in your niche, the area you have decided to focus on.

In the niche-building stage, you move your attention to a specific occupational area and interact with people to build your reputation in it. You strive to be seen as a professional with relevant, specific accomplishments and so will be more successful in a job interview. When asked what you have been doing since your last job, you will be ready to present a list of impressive, focused activities. This is also called building your brand.

In building a professional niche, you will:

- Emphasize the side of you that shows that you fit into the professional niche.

- Identify and meet contacts in a specific area who can provide mentorship and support.

- Acquire additional knowledge and skills in a specific segment within an occupational area.

- Interact in professional venues, such as online forums and in-person conferences, to meet people who are functioning successfully in the niche.

- Form partnerships to learn, share, find support, and become more visible.

- Obtain experiences, such as internships, and perform accomplishments that will build your reputation and your portfolio.

Formal schooling provides the same kind of bridge, but it is not always feasible and not always the best option. As a new graduate, you still need to go through the networking steps to focus in and to obtain relevant experience.

## *CULTURE BRIDGING*

An occupation is a culture. Part of developing depth in an occupational niche involves fitting into its unwritten and un-verbalized norms. So an important part of niche building is learning these norms and building personality habits that signal that you fit into the culture of your targeted field.

Everyone has carried out a wide variety of actions in past jobs, educational programs, community experiences, social interactions, and leisure activities. People tend to group their actions by the roles in which they performed them with further breakdowns into competencies. When we look back, we see labels for the abilities and interests we have expressed in those past experiences. For example, salespeople use empathy and leading questions to connect with and bring out needs from their prospects. The competency might be called "eliciting needs." Counselors also use the same methods, but the role and labels associated with those techniques for sales may preclude someone from seeing the use of the same talents in the role of a counselor or therapist. The way forward, then, if a person wants to build niche in counseling, moves from the labels and culture of sales to the labels and culture of counseling.

We now want to look into the future and package our actions in different ways that will fit our new vision. Removing our actions from the confines of our old structures and rearranging them—emphasizing previously downplayed actions over others, pulling in new ones to try out, discarding worn out or tired actions—allows us to see ourselves operating in new roles. New possibilities open up. This process involves recognizing old categories, which channel our attention to the past, and breaking down the walls that have grown up in our heads, which limit what we think we can do.

Open your eyes and ears to a new culture. Our occupations and our workplaces consist of people and programs that use abilities and knowledge to fill an economic need. In this system, we have become part of a culture with recognizable characteristics, including ways of working and ways of communicating with certain words and mannerisms. But if we continue to hold onto those ways of operating, we will limit our possibilities as the environment changes around us. Companies will—and must—adapt to changing conditions, and they will attract people who can adapt with them. If we want to stay an active participant in the ever-changing business world, we must reach into new territory, adopting the culture of new communities and assimilating new knowledge, abilities, mannerisms, language, and voice.

Additional cultural differences include the kind of management expected, the kinds of friendships that employees form, the level of humor allowed in business meetings, the amount of time permitted for people to talk about their families, and whether merit is openly recognized. An example of potential cultural conflict is when a person moves from the profit corporate world to a non-profit organization.

### Culture Adaptation

*In her job as a third grade special education teacher, Chris expressed care and compassion to children, but she had also developed assertiveness in dealing with a roomful of active students. Her strong personality complemented her physically active lifestyle, and after five years in the same position, Chris wanted to explore her career options. Her stories brought out an interest and ability in developing curriculum. In her networking activities, she began to interact with manufacturing organizations, discussing training activities. Her mannerisms moved from those tailored to talking with elementary school children to those attuned to influencing people in a manufacturing environment. Instead of bending down to the other person's eye level and patting them on the back, she stood tall and influenced people by stating her opinions strongly and clearly. Chris moved from being seen as belonging in an elementary school culture to being seen as credible in a manufacturing environment, and she found a satisfying job with a manufacturing organization filled with strong-willed engineers.*

## RÉSUMÉ FOR NICHE BUILDING

Your exploring résumé described in the last chapter emphasized your personality competencies that could be used in a number of occupations. Now that you have identified a niche within an occupation where you will be able to perform your best work, you need to "recast" your résumé to show how your competencies and accomplishments apply to that specific area.

You convey your focus by first showing the reader the specific occupational functions you want to perform and the evidence that conveys your expertise. When looking at the rest of the résumé, the reader, remembering what you listed at the top, will connect that information to the rest and think of you as an expert in those functions. Education and professional activities and interests follow.

*New Career Focus*

*Sandy rejuvenated his career at mid-life with a masters program in organizational development. Once he had completed the program, he carried out exploratory networking in which he considered all of the options in which his degree could be utilized, including specific areas within OD that best used his motivation. His niche building began with some pro-bono work for a government community-building project. Sandy gained further exposure to his chosen field by serving on a committee in a professional association. He found some traction in the area of communities of practice, where he could use his past experience in IT as well as his communication and facilitation skills.*

The following résumé introduces this focus to others.

# Niche-building Résumé

Sandy Blake
1099 Admiral Way, Seattle, WA, 98209,
sandyblake@hotmail.com, 206-469-0810

## Areas of Expertise

**Communities of Practice.** As a board member of a professional association, identified information needs of members and influenced the establishment of special interest groups to share knowledge. Our groups went far beyond normal activities to exchange information, and deep learning occurred.

**Organizational and Community Communication.** Surveyed members of an administrative office team to identify issues preventing improved sharing of information. During the feedback process, several people achieved insights, resulting in significant, positive changes in their performance. Member and leader for multiple development efforts involving governmental organizations.

**Information Systems Analysis.** Developed functional specifications for the budget, interviewing users and middle management, listening, and researching/ understanding the bigger picture.

## Relevant Work History

Consultant, Community Development Initiative,
Snohomish County, WA, 2004–2006

Information Systems Analyst, Lockheed Corporation,
Los Angeles, CA, 1997–2003

Counselor, Career Opportunities Center,
Bellevue, WA, 2007–2008

Teacher, IT and Web Design,
Various Community/Technical Colleges, 1988–1995

## Education

MA, Systems Consulting and Counseling, Martin University

BA Psychology, Evergreen State College

### Interests and Activities

SIG Leader, OD Network, Community communications projects

## THIRTY-SECOND COMMERCIAL

The same formula for the thirty-second commercial in options discovery applies to niche building: a sentence about your background, the competencies you want to use, and the kind of help you need. But, the content and the words are different. Instead of a summary of your complete background, apply your experience to the niche. Instead of all of your priority competencies, just mention those that apply to your niche and add some specific ones. You might have time to give an example. And instead of wanting to meet people who can help with options, look for people who can help you with your niche.

> "I have seven years experience interacting with people to identify business practices, two years involvement with organization facilitation projects, and seven years experience as a teacher. I want to use the knowledge management and leadership skills I demonstrated there to help an organization establish communities of practice. For example, the groups I ran were highly participative and had high rapport. I hope to meet people involved in knowledge management in organizations or elsewhere."

## HELPFUL ATTITUDES

**Inquisitiveness.** After having looked at your self, your past, the industry, and more to decide on a niche to pursue, you still need to keep exploring. Each occupational niche contains an incredible depth of information, possibilities, connections to other positions, etc. Learning what it holds never ends; your education, formal or not, should continual as long as you remain interested in that area. This is especially important for someone who is becoming a more specifically defined professional.

    **Investing.** Respond to every suggestion with eagerness to learn and to contribute. This could be volunteering for an association project with no obvious direct connection. If nothing else, you will be learning the culture and meeting people.

**Confidence in Continual Learning.** You may encounter some intimidating learning challenges, but you have already demonstrated your ability to learn new skills, concepts, mannerisms, or whatever the situation called for. Your past successes serve as reminders that you will continue to find success and give you reason for confidence about your learning in the future.

**Results Orientation.** In networking for discovering your options, described above, you talk about new ideas for their own sake. In a building a position in a professional niche, you need to pay more attention to the bottom line. Think about how you can do something that will show results in a specific area.

## INITIATING A DISCUSSION

Because talking with people to stay up-to-date is essential for professionals, niche-building discussions are much easier to carry out. You are a professional with experiences with new knowledge, talking with a fellow professional with the same kind of need. You might be open to having a mentor, and established professionals love to mentor.

## MESSAGE TO A NEW CONTACT

**Explain the connection.** If you got the person's name through searching a social networking site, say so.

> "Your Profile on Facebook indicates that you are helping organizations to improve efficiency of their operations."

**Present your own situation.** You have only a few words to convey your background.

> "Operations consulting is a niche I am building subsequent to my departure from a major aerospace manufacturer."

**State an example of your qualifications.** Examples provide the best possible credibility.

"In my work as a program executive, I always had an eye for opportunities to streamline operations. In one situation, I worked through people to collect some ideas, and through my good relationships, I saved processing time and dollars. In the past few months, I have had the opportunity to create similar efficiencies as an operations consultant to school districts."

**Present your request.** If your message states your goal clearly, you will be seen as efficient and not likely to waste the other's time.

"Would you be able to meet with me, either in person or by phone, for a brief discussion? You may have some ideas about how I can develop myself as an operations consultant. And you may know of professional groups or training opportunities that I can take advantage of."

**Express thanks and suggest next step, if appropriate.** If you have the other's phone number, you have the option of saying that you are planning a call. If you only have an email, you can only ask for a reply.

"Thanks in advance for your time and effort in helping. Please let me know if it's possible to talk. "

## MESSAGE TO A CURRENT CONTACT

**Reinforce connection.** If possible, convey that you are putting into practice the advice of the other person.

"Subsequent to our discussion of a few months ago, I have engaged in projects as an operations consultant ."

**Present reason.** Recognize the other person's interest in you, and also reinforce that you have something valuable to contribute.

"I would like to share my progress and also to let you know about some interesting client situations."

**Make a request.** Be specific.

"Is it possible to talk briefly by phone next week?"

**Express thanks and close.**

"Thanks. I appreciate your help in this and am looking forward to a brief conversation. If you give me a time and a phone number, I will give you a call."

## *Conversation for Niche Building*

Once you have secured a time for a phone call or a meeting, you take on a different tact with the other person. You now must build a relationship based on common professional interests and goals. You are no longer the humble searcher you were in requesting time to talk; now, you have a clear intention. But you are still doing everything possible to draw the other person out, to listen, and to make relevant statements. So, integrating questions into what you say is key. Here are the steps.

**Set the stage, situation, and thanks.** Remind the person about how the meeting evolved and your common interest.

"I was referred to you through one of my friends in the OD Network who is also involved in knowledge management. I am looking for ways to get involved in projects. Thanks for taking time to speak with me."

**Make a statement about your professional experience.** Show your experience and strong interest in making an impact in this niche.

"I had an opportunity to sit in on an introduction to a maintenance team and co-facilitated a sharing session."

**Get the other person talking and elicit more.** Listen to what the other person will volunteer before you lead the conversation. Show your ability to think on your feet through follow-up questions.

"What is happening in the profession from your point of view?"

"Where are the current opportunities?"

**Acknowledge and reinforce.** Your goal is to hit the other person's sweet spot, the place they love to talk about, and then let him or her give more on the topic.

> "That's a good insight. Tell me more."

**Initiate with expertise examples.** Show how you have been successfully involved and tack on a question about where that is happening.

> "I saw an article saying that the norms of the groups evolve in a very unique way in each group, and I am trying to find more examples of why that is important. Have you seen that?"

**Make leading statements.** The flow of the discussion can be helped if you lead it through insights.

> "Do you see activities in the structure of knowledge management that go along with communities of practice?"

**Have questions ready.** Show that you have spent time in researching what is happening by asking some well thought-out questions.

> "An article in *Wired* magazine discussed possible intellectual property issues in knowledge management. What are companies doing to create policies to avoid problems?"

## BUILDING REPUTATION

Your profile and résumé only hint at your reputation but serve to get you in the right door. Once you pass through it, your reputation depends on what you say and do. Now with your careful attention, it will develop more purposefully during your niche-building stage than it did before.

When your competencies and profile align with your true self and you enter the door, you naturally want to give expression to your self. What you have accomplished, how you have done it, the results your actions have generated, how others perceive you and your work all contribute to your reputation; it best expresses who you are to those around you. And, if your efforts have created a good reputation, it will attract the right people to you

Activities that build your reputation can include the following:

- Leadership in a professional association
- Research to stay up-do-date on the latest thinking
- Internships with leaders
- Participation in Internet groups and dialogues
- Blogging
- Providing work samples

## PROFESSIONAL COMMUNITIES

Professional communities are an ideal forum for interacting with others who can help you to continue your career path in an ideal direction. Professional associations organized around a specific occupation and trade associations organized around industries have a long history of:

- Organizing conferences and workshops for presenting and exchanging ideas.
- Identifying and offering educational content for professional development.
- Holding meetings to present information and facilitate connections.
- Sponsoring Special Interest Groups (SIGs) in which innovative ideas are explored in depth.

Search the Gateway to Associations database sponsored by the Association of Association Executives at http://www.asaecenter.org/Community/Directories/associationsearch.cfm.

The Internet has spawned many professional communities that are not modeled after the traditional professional association format. Their goal is to be a central resource of information and interaction. Create a search phrase by combining an occupational area with certain words. For example:

- knowledge management +expertise
- process improvement + "professional community"

As a result of engaging in a professional community, your career will prosper because you will have the opportunity to:

- Meet new people who will be able to tell you what is happening inside of and outside of organizations.

- Build leadership skills and make contacts by being part of a team that organizes events.

- Build your expertise through educational events and meetings.

- Use your talents in a way that can enhance your resume.

## *BLOGGING*

The potential of the Internet for helping people connect is immense. The following chapter presents the use of social networks in meeting people and exchanging ideas in connection with a career and work search. At this time, blogs, short for "Web logs," are the primary way in which professionals interact. They are created and monitored by an individual with a personal interest in a topic. They are easy to set up and are easily found. The originator discusses a topic, others are able to make comments to share their ideas, and new knowledge is created. Strong reputations have been built in the political and entertainment arenas through the use of blogs.

However, they are not fostering the discussions they could among other professionals. Very few people bother to make a comment—and this creates a wonderful opportunity for you to stand out. Finding interesting blogs and making comments is a good way to engage a fellow professional. Ideally, you would also be building a reputation among a group of professionals and future employers.

Google has a search tool specifically for blogs. It has identified content on blogging sites at locations with blog in the address and at many other locations where ideas are presented and comments allowed and encouraged. The blogs with the most recent updates are returned

first. With their caffeine technology, the results can be sorted by a
number of timeframe options. Here are some examples:

Entered: C# Programming

> Found: http://forum.codecall.net/c-programming/23353-
> c-regular-expressions.html

> This is a site at which code ideas are exchanged.

Entered: advertising account management

> Found: http://brandinsightblog.com/2009/07/06/garbage-in-
> garbage-out-%E2%80%94-how-to-get-effective-advertising-
> from-your-agency/

> This is an exchange of ideas for managing advertising
> campaigns.

Entered: knowledge management

> Found: http://it.toolbox.com/blogs/managing-infosec/

> This is an exchange of ideas for managing knowledge
> through IT.

Entered: quality assurance

> Found: http://www.chinaqualityassurance.com/from-quality-
> assurance-to-communication-5-elements-of-efficient-
> project/#respond

> This site has ideas for improving communication.

Entered: medical research

> Found: http://www.sla.org/

> This site creates dialogue for researching results of projects.

Entered: educational policy

> Found: http://rickosbornscontinuingeducationblog.blogspot.
> com/2009/12/maybe-you-should-consider-video-games.html

These are articles and comments overseen by someone with a contribution to make.

Entered: supply chain management

> Found: http://www.communities.hp.com/online/blogs/manufacturing-distribution/default.aspx

> A person could get a good start in the manufacturing/distribution arena with these ideas.

Entered: marketing technical products

> Found: http://www.workingmemo.com/viral-marketing-traffic-power/

> This information is available in a rapid way, increasing its benefit.

Entered: communities of practice

> Found: http://blog.mountaingoatsoftware.com/the-fallacy-of-one-throat-to-choke

> These results of experience are made available to a wide audience thanks to Internet blogs.

## WORK SAMPLES

The elements you use in finding a job reflect but a part of you and merely substitute for the real thing—your work. Résumés present past job titles and employers, summarize your duties, and highlight your accomplishments. But they are not the real thing. You have spent hours selecting words to portray you at your best. Job interviews show you interacting with work issues while you are on your best behavior. References present a similar side of you. But none of those elements come near meaning as much as the real thing—your work.

When you are known by the fruits of your labor, your work, you will feel fairly represented and appreciated. In many cases, you will have produced results that both you and your employer want known publicly and given recognition for accomplishing. In some cases your employer may restrict what you display because of a need for product secrecy.

With search engines able to identify very detailed information, having samples online may attract people who will help you and your company to move forward. For instance, companies looking for software code often find it online and then employ its creator.

Graphic artists and designers have made excellent use of work samples. Now, with the Internet, even those outside the art-related fields can take advantage of making their work samples available to others and thus giving wider display of their reputation. Work samples can take the form of text, pictures, graphics, or videos.

**Text.** Proposals, marketing descriptions, software code, and research results will add to your career credibility. Testimonials especially give credence to your good reputation.

**Pictures.** A picture of your work team at a social function will convey warmth and teamwork. You might want a picture of a product you sell or designed or your involvement in a service you provide, such as a happy class during one of your training sessions.

**Graphics.** A flow chart of a business system gives an immediate overview. A mind map will create in the viewer the same expanded feeling that it creates in you.

**Videos.** Entering "work sample +marketing" into YouTube brings up an ad for a video company. Soon, many kinds of products will be promoted in the same way. Your career products can be among them.

We have identified several major ways of building a professional reputation, all of which you can continue to do throughout your career and not just when searching for work.

- Have you ever spent a day doing nothing but developing your professional expertise? If not, why not? Do you think you will be able to do that now?

- If you are in this stage now, or when you reach this stage, do you think that you will be able to develop skills and knowledge and to gain experience so that you can keep up with the leaders in the field?

- When you are at this stage, what percentage of the week do you think should be spent on development?

# Networking to Market Yourself as a Consultant

Besides giving substance to your reputation, working for an organization as a consultant also provides one of the major ways of landing a good job with that organization. The percentage of people you see in a workplace who work as consultants and not employees has been growing during the last twenty years. This means increased opportunity but less security for individuals and greater access to new ideas but less employee loyalty for organizations.

During your exploring and niche building, you have talked with people representing various occupations and possessing different accomplishments. They exposed you to a variety of views about the best way to perform in an occupational area and maybe even what not to do. This is perfect training for a consultant, a person who looks at a situation in a new way and applies the most appropriate skills to get the task done with finesse.

Consultant marketing differs from a traditional marketing effort where the emphasis is on the dissemination of information. Just as in effective work finding, consultant marketing involves getting the other person talking, listening, making leading statements, asking questions and building upon the responses, and showing expertise by relating stories of accomplishment. Consultant marketing extends these methods by directing attention to the situation of the potential customer. The key question posed at the right time is: "Would a proposal be appropriate?" The consultant who initiates this kind of request will probably be the only person submitting one and thus have no competition. In other situations, the company may publish a formal Request for a Proposal (RFP), and many potential consultants would respond. The consultant who already has had a conversation about the need will have an obvious advantage.

## CONSULTANT MARKETING RÉSUMÉ

The following marketing résumé summarizes at the top the person's most relevant qualifications. Then, persuasive highlights in the functional areas of the person's expertise follow. Last, the work history and professional involvement add support.

In this sample, Randy transitioned from an executive role. In the first few months, he explored potential opportunities as an operations executive as his new status became known among his social contacts and as he inquired about possibilities. His niche-development activities were to apprentice with a consulting firm, which had business in operations improvement. Now he is taking the initiative in contacting the presidents of small organizations to both identify possible consulting opportunities and express an interest in a possible employment capacity.

His résumé shows some projects that might match the needs of many small businesses. If a president he approaches does not see a direct need, he or she might have a related one, and Randy's résumé makes a connection to such a need. It provides one page of information to motivate a person with needs in operations to discuss them with Randy.

**Consultant Marketing Résumé**

Randy Olson
3094 Forest Ave., Rochester, NY 14618, rolson@msn.com, 585-687-3287

### Summary of qualifications

- Over 20 years successful experiences understanding the dynamics of complex situations and improving organizational processes and functional performance.
- Clients include leading educational and services organizations.
- Built and led participative teams for strategizing and problem solving.
- Prior executive-level responsibility for a major manufacturer.

### Project Highlights

**Needs Identification.** Led staff analysis for military program status involving identifying complex benchmarks. Interacted with organization's leadership to identify critical needs and management's plan of action. Conducted interviews and analyzed operations to surface overall issues for recommended improvements.

**Surveys.** Developed, conducted, and analyzed organization's surveys on customer satisfaction; recommended action plans addressing specific issues. Conducted employee interviews intended to establish overall organizational climate as it related to leadership performance, interpersonal relationships, and morale issues.

**Analysis of Organizational Structure.** Reviewed and analyzed organizational workflow for operational efficiency and opportunities to improve organization's interaction and overall structure.

**Operations Analysis.** Examined school district's support operations (maintenance, warehousing, food service, payroll services, etc.) to establish quantitative opportunities and recommended actions for efficiency and effectiveness.

### Work History

2002–2009 Program Manager, Major Air Force Program, General Dynamics
1999–2002 Program Manager, Missile Division, Raytheon
1997–1999 Deputy Program Manager, Lockheed
1983–1995 Sales and Marketing, Honeywell Marine Systems

### Education

MBA, Management, University of Washington
B.S., Mechanical Engineering, Georgia Institute of Technology

### Professional Activities and Interests

Committee member of American Association of Quality Control

## THIRTY-SECOND COMMERCIAL

This is an opportunity to highlight what you do best and convey that your skills enable you to undertake a wide variety of projects. Be specific about your directly related background and summarize your work that touched on your target market area when you were in other kinds of jobs. Tell a good story in a few sentences about an accomplishment. Seek to meet people who are engaged in the specific market area and can hire you.

> "In my thirty years in program and executive management positions with a major manufacturer, I was effective in improving operational efficiency. In one situation, I worked through ten project managers and made major budget reductions while keeping morale high. I have recently used popular methodologies to improve efficiency in educational organizations, and I am able to apply the principles to many kinds of organizational issues. I am looking for an opportunity to talk with managers in need of greater efficiency or information about a current proposal process."

## HELPFUL ATTITUDES

**Knowledge Resource.** In a consultant role, you remain outside the inner circle of the organization. This position puts you at an advantage in the way those in that circle see you—as a professional with important insight, analysis, and knowledge to share—and keeps you from needing to understand how to function within that particular organization.

**Work through People.** An outside consultant has no power except through an ability to influence people. Your effectiveness in this arena depends upon your awareness of others' attitudes, your responses to them, and your motivational and teaching skills.

**Service and Attentiveness.** You communicate respect by focusing totally on the other person's agenda. Rather than subservience, you demonstrate the ultimate wisdom.

**Adaptability.** A successful consultant simply does what is needed. With an open mind, he or she communicates clearly and comes up with an out-of-the-box solution.

## REACHING OUT

To find a position as a consultant, begin by tactfully contacting your current network. Check out LinkedIn and Facebook. Your resources in either one may be connected to a person who is looking for a person just like you.

Part of the job of managers involves keeping up-to-date on what is happening in their field, and their quickest review of credible people comes from scanning the mountains of printed material that appears in their in-box. The focus and quality of the materials convey the kind of organization that is sending it, and although the quality of your mailing will not match many in that group, you do need to have your information in that pile. So for your next step, you will create a mailing via snail mail. Because it takes more time and effort than the alternative, managers will value the thought and effort that went into the mailing over a simple-to-write email. They will probably not see you in the same league as the high-end consultants, but a letter with your consultant résumé may catch the eye of someone looking for innovative ideas that are not stuck in a glossy brochure.

## APPROACH MESSAGE

This is the same as a sales letter. Organizations get many of them, so be brief and make an effort to stand out.

**Bridge from what is on their mind to the kind of discussion you would like to have.** You have to have some insights into your niche to know what issues to address, to know what their concerns are, to guess accurately what they are looking for.

"Many organizations are discovering that the innovations that arise from continual improvement never end."

**Build your credibility.** Assume that they have poorly defined issues, which makes predicting a solution strategy near impossible. So, give an example of both identifying a real problem and facilitating an unexpected solution.

> "Devising good solutions requires, first, precisely defining the problems. I have done both. In one instance, I identified unspoken priorities and motivated team members to create ideas for increased productivity."

**Make a request.** Everything starts with a conversation. Those with responsibility for making something happen recognize that their role is to engage in conversations and to lead in acting on the results.

> "Would you be interested in discussing how the newest ideas in team and productivity improvement can be applied to your situation?"

**Give more on your background.** If you have included a project summary, use it to make your case.

> "As you can see from the enclosed project summary, I have successes in situations such as yours."

**Assume success.** This is not imposing. It's acting from a place of abundance. You have good ideas, and they have good ideas, and the best idea brings them together.

> "I'll call to arrange a brief discussion unless I hear from you. Thanks in advance for making room in your busy schedule."

One of the obstacles to success in networking is that many believe they are intruding in a way that will work against their job-searching efforts. However, that obstacle does not exist with consultant marketing. Just like thousands of other organizations, in your mailing you are getting the word out about the services you have to offer.

## DISCUSSION FORMAT

In a consultative selling approach, the salesperson's skill brings out key information from the other person and then uses it to make the sale. Neil Rackham has identified four stages of this approach with the acronym SPIN: Situation, Problem, Implication, Need. Smart salespeople use the sequence to raise a strongly felt need in their prospect. First, for the situation, salespeople get the other to describe a situation that isn't working. Second, for the problem, they ask questions that help to analyze the situation to determine the cause. No emotions come into play at this point, only an objective review. Third, for the implication, salespeople draw out the emotions that the other feels about the situation and its cause when its implication is fully realized. Last, for the need, salespeople connect the emotions to a need that their product or service will satisfy. At this point, the prospect is ready to hear—and more likely accept—the salesperson's idea.

A consultant marketing discussion can use a similar sequence.

**Build a relationship and provide opening bridge.** Show your interest in having an interesting, two-way interaction.

> "Thanks for having your feelers out and being willing to have a discussion about performance improvement. I have read that innovation is important to you."

**Question to elicit information about the other's situation.** The other person might have a problem or issue on his or her mind that prompted calling you. With appropriate questioning on your part, you may discover it and connect your expertise to solving it. Give the other the opportunity to open with that.

> "What specific approach have you found works for you?"

**Make leading statement and attach a question.** You need to have an idea that likely applies to that organization. You mention it to get the person to open up a little about the real issues, but if he or she doesn't, you need to have a question ready to go.

"Productivity varies greatly within each group. Have you found a specific approach that brings everyone up to the same level?"

"As you know, employee ownership of innovations occurs when all employees contribute to the ideas. How has that worked here?"

**Identify and expand the problem.** Use active listening to suggest a productive avenue for discussion. Encourage sharing.

"From what you are saying, it seems as if your employees need greater awareness of the bigger picture. Could you talk more about that?"

**Build a realization of implications.** You want to move awareness of the problem from the person's head to the heart so he or she feels connected to an outcome and wants to take action.

"What is the implication of that? How does it affect your time to market"?

**Reinforce the need and create action.** In an ideal scenario, the other person tells you the kind of project he or she envisions, and you feed the ideas back.

"What kind of project do you have in mind?"

"Would you like to see how that would look as a project? What kind of information would you like to see in a proposal?"

Carrying out consultant marketing can have a powerful impact on your career. It allows you to describe yourself in the best light, to talk at greater length about what you have to offer, and to stand with other professionals who offer similar services. You are making a mental intention every time you send out a mailing, whether a letter, a mini brochure, or a more extensive brochure. You are spending about half your time on it. You are feeling risk, expanding your comfort zone, and confronting self-doubt, all of which are the ingredients of success.

Consultant marketing helps you focus your efforts mentally as well as physically. Channeling your thoughts into a single purpose creates energy that brings more energy to you. You operate like a magnet, drawing to you people and events and opportunities that will contribute to your success. In contrast, when you are working in a mere job rather than work that truly defines you, you send out less positive signals. Only part of your whole being contributes to the job; the rest is fighting the situation. In a similar manner, when you are looking for a job, you scatter your energy, giving some to one activity, some to your current job, some to another potential employer. Without a single-minded focus, these efforts lack intensity. But in consultant marketing, as you draw more of what you need to you, you reinforce your efforts, do more to keep the momentum going, and further strengthen your magnetic pull.

In consulting marketing, you implement a selling model to meet new people and to continue the process of building a presence in the workplace. This kind of follow-through builds momentum and brings opportunity.

- Have you sold your services before? What emotional reaction did you have as a result? Did it give you energy and momentum?

- Do you feel that you can adapt to fill a variety of needs in your overall niche area?

- Do you have an accomplishment you can refer to in your marketing?

<br />
<br />

<br />

CHAPTER TEN

# INTERNET SOCIAL NETWORKING

The sign of career security has always been an employment history of jobs with increasing responsibility with respected organizations. Now we have another symbol: a pyramid of people. The best security possible comes from connections with people. Internet social networks such as LinkedIn, Facebook, and Twitter automate the process of finding and meeting the people who are the essential link between you and an opportunity for rewarding work. On LinkedIn, your current contacts are called Level 1 contacts. Their direct contacts are Level 2 contacts for you. The direct contacts of the Level 2 contacts are Level 3 contacts for you. Each successive level has more people. Combined, they form a pyramid structure that has the potential to make you, the person at the top, a success.

## LINKEDIN

Employment professionals created LinkedIn to facilitate career building and job finding. Companies enter job openings, and individuals find out about them and apply for them. At the same time, the applicant automatically receives information if someone in his or her pyramid network is employed at the company. If one is found, then the people-connection and idea-generation/discussion capability of LinkedIn come into play. The applicant can join groups that the person is in and might engage in enough compatible professional development activities to warrant a meeting for a conversation. As a result, the person could feel a commonality of business interests, might influence HR to give the applicant's résumé extra attention, and could bring the person to the attention of the hiring manager.

Career counselors and coaches throughout the nation are reporting successful use of LinkedIn.

A job seeker scoured his connections and found someone who worked for a company to which he was applying for a job in IT. He emailed the person he knew and asked if she would ask her connection if an email or phone communication with him was possible. It was, and so they both emailed and talked on the phone. He subsequently was interviewed.

A programmer used the LinkedIn search engine to find people employed at a company he was interested in working for, SAP. He found that a professor from his MBA program was linked to a department director in the company. He used the LinkedIn function designed to make introductions of people once removed and so was able to communicate with the director. The director forwarded his résumé to IT, and he was hired.

A client making a career change was able to get the information she needed by networking with people both from her LinkedIn pyramid and from others.[1]

While job finding is facilitated by LinkedIn, users would better focus on its career-building processes of creating a network based on trust. Then they will have interacted with those professional connections in a positive way before they learn about a job. LinkedIn enables career searchers and work finders to engage in conversations about professional development that are beneficial, but this can come about only if both parties trust the other. When trust exists, people are willing to share information with others they do not know directly.

## *PROFILE*

LinkedIn organizes its profile to elicit quickly from you and present to people who visit your page the most essential information needed for connecting. This overview puts the most important information at the top and gives you an opportunity to expand further down the page. That means that visitors to your page get a quick, succinct overview of you, and if they want to learn more, they can scroll down the page. All of the descriptive information you enter in your profile will be used in the People Search to help others find you. Following, in bold, are the headings in the profile that you will find especially helpful.

**Personal Headline.** Citizens' band radio users first conceived of the idea of a "handle." It's amazing how much a headline of only two or three words can convey about a person. Sometimes creative types put together words in innovative ways: Proactive Project Manager, Visionary Executive, and Efficient Administrator all say tons about a person.

**Summary:** Make your summary action-oriented so that your readers will want to take action when they see your message. Begin with: "I want to use …" Present your priority competencies and give an example. For example, you can say "I want to use my competencies in public relations and organizing community events to improve an organization's relationship with its public. My organizing and promoting a concert increased inquiries about one of our promotional events. As a writer, I edited and was a writer for a newsletter that received over 100 requests to subscribe." Use the summary to present the roles you want to play and in which you have experience. Summarize your priority activities and accomplishments. Do not just repeat information about your job titles that is above and below.

**Specialties.** This lists your functional expertise in title form. You would include descriptors, such as Knowledge Management, Editor, Writer, Events Promoter, Process Improvement, Team Building, Group Facilitation. The words are similar to the key word summary on your résumé.

**Recommendations.** Recruiters working both inside companies and for fees independently who are intensely searching for candidates for job openings place high value on recommendations. Their use of LindedIn for this search benefits job seekers, who no longer have to locate contact information about recruiters and mail letters and résumés individually to each one. LinkedIn also provides the means for your asking people in your network for a recommendation, which it calls an "endorsement."

**Contact Advice.** Be realistic about how active you can be. If you are busy, say so. If you are eager for new projects because you are between jobs, be clear. If you are looking for job openings only, be broad about the kinds of openings you are considering.

## DISCOVERING NEW OPTIONS

Searching on "People" on LinkedIn brings the capability of looking at all of the words in a person's profile. A searcher can enter his or her own competency words and discover others who used the same ones in their Profile. The individual can then look at the others' current and former occupations to help discover where those who have been in the same occupation have gone in their career or found employment.

Entering "out of the box thinking" brought the occupations of advertising manager, special projects manager, emerging technologies product manager, and entertainment CEO.

Entering "relating with empathy" brought IT support, attorney, research analyst, dementia care company owner, financial services sales, health-wellness-fitness consultant, and an elementary special education teacher.

Entering "take risks" brought international trade development, compliance specialist, PR, management, advertising coordinator, and marketing consultant.

## CONNECTING WITH PEOPLE

When trust exists within a group, members assume that someone known by a current connection will interact with similar people in a positive and productive way. They will prepare and ask useful questions.

They will listen and make beneficial contributions in individual and group interactions. They will take a risk in advancing new idea. They will say yes to invitations to connect and talk. And they will willingly make referrals.

The best person you can converse with for information to help you in your career might be one of your past classmates or workmates. If that person is a member of LinkedIn, you will receive a suggestion to contact the person as soon as you create your profile. Your pyramid quickly builds because people you already know have contacts, and their contacts have contacts. They also compare the names in your address books to their current members and suggest more contacts. Suggestions of who to contact continue daily, and they build momentum.

Referrals are the grease that makes career advancement possible. Individuals can spend many hours researching occupations and industries and, in the process, discover people who can make helpful contacts. But how can you communicate with them? LinkedIn facilitates sending direct messages to Level 1 connections. From talking with my clients and others, I estimate that direct messaging to people you already know results in a discussion 95 percent of the time. LinkedIn provides a messaging process to help you make Level 2 connections by routing a message through the Level 1 connection and suggesting a forwarding message. Counselors have told me that Level 2 and Level 3 connections are completed a high percentage of time if they are between middle-level managers/professionals and above, including CEOs. One reason they respond is that they typically use networking to accomplish some of their work. Level 2 and Level 3 connections between lower level technical employees, such as software developers, result in discussions less often, according to my contacts. In my experience, referral messaging by work finders to network connections works around 15 percent of the time. But direct messages with no connection in a relationship are much less effective. LinkedIn provides a specialized for-pay service called Inmail that has proven effective in setting up conversations with people to whom you have no connection 30 percent of the time.

Your developing connections with professional colleagues in the LinkedIn network requires action on your part, in addition to reading and sending messages. One activity that eliminates the layers of connections is to become a member of a group since members can message each other directly. In the past, just discovering an appropriate association gave cause for celebration; now, the Internet makes many relevant groups readily available. LinkedIn now has thousands of groups on a wide variety of topics that can be used to learn about what is happening in an occupational area, pass on useful information, and match up people who are able to help each other.

They have groups in these categories: alumni, corporate, conference, networking, non-profit, professional, and other. You can enter your city into the search for groups so that you can browse for a one that might result in a local contact. Searching for groups in LinkedIn brought the following results.

Entered: advertising

> Returned: 2,923 groups differing by location and kind of media

Entered: operations improvement

> Returned: 26 groups for specific improvement processes, such as Kaizen and Six Sigma, and for various industries.

Entered: sales

> Returned: 6,709 groups around skill improvement and industry

Entered: supply chain

> Returned: 1,613 groups around industries and specific roles

Entered: health care

> Returned: 1,363 groups for specific functions within health care

Entered: travel

> Returned: 2,428 groups for segments and kinds of clients

Entered: entertainment

Returned: 1,874 groups around job function

Occupational literature has general information about how to plan a career path for an occupation. However, it rarely provides information about whether a person with specific and out-of-the-ordinary experiences will succeed in making it. Social networks feature very powerful searches that can reveal opportunities that the standard literature neglects. Someone wondering whether a person with a similar background can advance need only enter that past job and a new occupation into a search and identify whether anyone else has made such a move. Of course, in these times of rapid change moves into unchartered territory are made all of the time, and so don't let the fact that no one has made such a career change hold you back.

The same principles and skills that make personal networking successful hold equal importance for interacting on the social networking scene. These include tactful approaching, envisioning possibilities, sending messages that lead to conversations, talking about strengths effectively, asking interesting and insightful questions, listening, and drawing people out in a way that engages them.

## FACEBOOK

Do you like to connect with people or connect with friends from the past? If you have not already, go to www.facebook.com, and reacquaint yourself with old friends and extend your network of connections worldwide. When you sign up, Facebook searches your email address book for people already on Facebook and suggests that you contact them, giving you a start on a friend's group. Many people use Facebook to keep each other informed about what they are feeling, thinking, and doing with one text entry and click. You and your friends might exchange information about a movie you've seen or a hike you took by making an entry into your status text box, or you might initiate a discussion that will result in a future outing.

You can make a post that your friends will see by sharing interesting information about yourself. In turn, you will know what your friends are doing by reading their pages. And you all will be interested because you share in the experience of being connected. But be careful. Connecting this easily comes with a risk. Employers now routinely check out the Web presence of their job candidates. You do not want them to find a picture or a video which might cast you in a negative light.

You decide who sees the information in the text box at the top of the page. You can limit viewers of what you say only to you, to you and your friends, or to you and everyone who visits your page and all of the Internet.

The profile that you build contains information that Facebook uses to suggest people as your friends. The basis for the suggested connections includes your listed hometown, schools, and jobs.

Facebook can help your career and job search. You can participate in a career-related group in which, for instance, you learn of ideas used in an occupation and discuss them. In the group, you will have a chance to interact with people new to you who might be able to help you. You can find a person working in a targeted company if he or she has opened the security settings and then learn whether he or she is connected to you through a friend.

In the profile, you list your location, schools, and jobs in a way similar to LinkedIn. An important addition here is that you can include pictures, videos, and notes. If you have pictures, videos or other graphical representations of your work, you can use them to increase your impact.

Facebook enables its members to create an ad targeted to specific people. A person who wanted to be a book publicist found people employed in publishing and created an ad targeted to them. It stated that she wanted to work for their firm, had a picture, and was linked to her résumé.[2]

# TWITTER

Knowledge does not move the world forward as much as the short comments about that knowledge from a fresh perspective that interprets it and applies it. And it doesn't take many words to contribute to an idea and then point to a place to learn more about it. It turns out that a very workable number of characters is 140, the maximum number allowed on a text message from a cell phone. The quickest way for a career and job searcher to find out the latest information about an occupation, investigate an idea, or meet a person with a common interest is to search the "tweets" made on Twitter. They will point the way for an engaging Web surfing journey.

You can identify whether your ideas will engage the work place and the economy by making a tweet and seeing if it generates interest and creates a following. You might simply make a referral to a good book on any topic. If your observation provides a new perspective or has some special aspect to it that appeals to others, it might start a conversation.

Begin by going to www.twitter.com and entering an occupational interest in the search box. The return you see will be messages three lines long that others have posted that contain your words and a link. At the top of the list will be a number of job ads. There will also be comments about your words, usually with a link to a blog or a Web site. Click on the link and you will be taken to the blog or Web site that contains the information. You can also click on the picture of the person who posted the tweet to be taken to his or her home page showing all of that person's recent tweets. There you can see who he or she is connected to and is following, leading you to more useful information.

The rapid success of Twitter testifies to the fact that the best information comes directly from people. A search on Google probably will not yield the same quality of information as quickly. With Twitter, both members and non-members see a large search box. Enter an occupation, a role within an occupation, or a product that interests you. The search won't return anything if it can't find all of the words in your search string. If you get no returns, take words out. Here are some examples:

Entered: humorous advertising

> Returned: a candidate, which means job seeker, from a name "hot candidates."

Entered: efficient code

> Returned: a person who talked about using software code efficiently on his project.

If you join, you will see a white menu bar at the upper right. There you can search for people who interest you and sign-up as a follower.

Using social networks to advance a job or career search proves especially beneficial in this country where we have the freedom to make new social connections of any kind. Social networks continually change, gaining and losing members, providing fresh contacts, opening up new opportunities. The excuse that you don't know the right people isn't true anymore.

Because the United States has no structured career choice and job finding system, everyone planning a career and finding work must utilize all of the methods available. Each person's success depends upon the individual and the effort expended. Social networks are a vital tool.

Your career success greatly depends upon your connecting with people, and Internet social networking provides an effective means to magnify your current number, level, and familiarity of contacts.

- Social networking enables you to meet people through additional channels. Who is an ideal person you would like to meet?

- The value of the information you get from people connected to you is higher than what you would get from a search on the entire Web. What kind of information do you want more of and what kind of person can give it to you?

- What social skills do you have that will be valuable in social networking?

CHAPTER ELEVEN

# WORK FINDING PERSISTENCE

Your next job will most likely be a positive step along your career path. It will enable you to use your interests and abilities to create some accomplishments that will support a better career future. It will be a step in the right direction. The key to your moving in that direction is persistence.

In looking at the stories of your experiences, you have become more aware of the degree to which the physical, emotional, intellectual, and non-physical parts of your personality are developed, accessible, and in play. Now as you engage the workplace, you need to use your whole personality, letting each aspect contribute its strength. Your physical side will take the lead when you walk around, prepare and post work samples, and stick to a schedule. Your emotional side will take over as you form bonds with others for a support network. Your intellectual side will manage when you research options and have professional discussions. And your non-physical side will guide as you become committed and inspired.

## ACTIVITY PLANNING

When you approach any endeavor and desire success, you must persist despite any roadblocks. This holds equally true in looking for a job, and persistence often involves implementing a variety of approaches. Richard Bolles has reviewed the research on the effectiveness of job finding methods. He discovered the following success rates for each listed method. (A range of percentages indicates that multiple people researched the method. Also, he does not separate the results by occupational type.)[1]

- Internet (putting a résumé into a résumé database and searching career sites and other places for job openings; applying online): 4-10%.
- Mailing résumés to employers at random: 7%
- Answering ads in trade journals: 7%
- Answering local newspaper ads: 5-24%
- Going to employment agencies: 5-28%
- Asking family, friends, or staff at career centers: 33%
- Knocking on the door of an employer of interest: 47%
- Working alone and directly contacting employers: 69%
- Contacting when in a job club group: 84%
- Carrying out a life-changing job hunt, which results in approaching a manager: 86%

Research by the Bureau of Labor Statistics shows that people who implement many job search methods rather than just one or two have greater success. The bureau also believes that one of the most effective job search methods is direct employer contact. It recommends that job seekers research desired employers, stay aware of advertised job openings, and find ways to contact people in the company regardless of whether a job is being advertised.

Following are some possible actions you might take during a week. Do them when you implement some of the recognized options above. First, identify the emotions each brings for you. If an activity fits your personality, it will feel natural, and you will likely implement it. If an activity brings some new information or a relationship that might help in the future, you will feel rewarded. If an activity pushes you beyond your comfort zone, you will need added energy to complete it. But you will likely need to embrace activities that both come easy to you and challenge you. Use the chart that follows the list to plan a week that balances activities that drain you with those that build you up. Here are possible activities.

- **Writing thank-you messages.** Do this immediately after each of your meetings. Do not delay. Each takes but a few minutes, and once done, it's done. Allocate time to insure you do it. The thank-you process brings positive feelings both to your contact and to yourself.

- **Making networking appointments.** If you are feeling out of options, the most productive action you can take is to initiate a personal connection. You will look at the positive side of things in identifying someone to approach. You will feel good after your discussion and will broaden your ideas about options and what you can do to engage them.

- **Conducting networking interviews.** These are the lifeblood of career growth. Talking about your positives builds confidence and listening to identify a new perspective broadens perceptions. Aim for three interviews per week.

- **Improving self-understanding.** One of the reasons that you might feel stuck is that you are not in touch with a feasible option. Understanding more about yourself, combined with looking outward with optimism, will bring more options into play.

- **Improving job-search materials, such as letters and résumés.** This activity is both reflective and physical and can be the first step towards other physical actions that will make something happen for you.

- **Putting work samples online.** You are expanding the ways users of your services can become aware of you.

- **Finding and applying to published jobs.** You will benefit from seeing needs and trends in the job market through the lens of job announcements. Do not be discouraged by the fact that extensive qualifications that are being requested. Companies advertise for the ideal and usually consider people with less. The process of fitting your experiences and strengths into a new situation can build flexibility and confidence.

- **Contacting potential employers' HR departments directly.** Many HR people actually want to remain in touch with a group of potential employees. For your method of contact, you may follow up on a job application by phone, or you might drop in to see if the company has a bulletin board with announcements.

- **Exploring by walking around a neighborhood.** This engages your whole being, including the physical, and can lead to positive momentum. You can make it part of your exercise routine.

- **Exploring through written resources.** Getting into the habit of doing some of this each week, for both exploring and niche building, will help you to keep up with the changing world.

- **Keeping in touch with your current network through progress letters.** Remember that other people want to keep a connection with you just as much as you do with them.

- **Writing grant applications and responding to RFPs.** If you are marketing yourself as a consultant, doing this will increase your awareness of workplace needs and the most advanced ways of meeting them. You will interact with potential colleagues as a part of preparing the proposal and possibly decide to partner for a stronger proposal.

- **Preparing consulting processes and materials.** At this stage, you have a network of supporters with whom you are maintaining contact, and this activity improves your competitiveness.

- **Working in an internship or project capacity, either in a for-pay or pro-bono arrangement.** This is one of the best ways to build your résumé and meet new people.

- **Building competencies.** Especially in times of change but also throughout your career, you need to attend to this. You will also meet new people and expand your horizons.

- **Phoning directly to hiring managers.** Think of a manager who is looking for ways to improve his department. How can you help?

- **Meeting with a support group.** Talking about your activities will get you some good ideas and help you move your search to the next level.

- **Being counseled or coached.** A different perspective will give you valuable insights and help you view your past, present, and future more favorably.

- **Spending time with family.** Look for and accept support from all channels; support is typically very beneficial.

- **Engaging in recreation.** This will keep energy, activity, and momentum flowing for you. Often, as the physical activity releases tension in the body, it makes room for good ideas to enter the mind.

- **Performing activities that engage the mind and body to reduce stress.** The benefits to your well-being of exercise, Pilates, yoga, qigong, or some other mind-body activity go beyond what recreation can offer.

Use the combination of methods that reflects the stage of your job search. If you are newly transitioned, and you still like your most recent job, you might use all possible methods to apply to ones just like it. You would respond to published ads, contact employers directly, and make direct phone calls to hiring managers. However, only using these methods would quickly drain your batteries because you may not get enough rewards to balance the effort you are expending. Add to those ones that will bring you more immediate and positive results. Make contacts with both people who can help you hone your professional knowledge and those who will help you explore.

If you want to take time to expand your career options, begin with both researching written information and networking with people to discover new opportunities. In interacting with people who provide support for your efforts, your values will strengthen, and you will add definition as a unique individual. At this point, you would hold off contacting potential employers until you have established a strong new direction.

Whatever your combination of career and work finding activities, it's beneficial to participate in balancing kinds of activities so that you manage your emotions and maintain a positive outlook. These other activities might include stress-reducing physical activity, family time, recreation, and meeting with a support group. The following chapter talks more about maintaining balance so that you will be at your best throughout your searching activity.

Plan your week to take into consideration your *internal* prime time which is the day of the week and the time of day that you will be at your best for a certain kind of activity. When is the best time of day for you to read and research because you can concentrate? When do you feel most energized and most strong within yourself that you can take on risks, such as making outreach calls? When do you feel most relaxed and comfortable with yourself so that meeting with other people goes smoothly? Do you have to dress well in the morning to make the day work, or are you more productive in your sweats? When are you creative and able to write imaginative letters? What kind of evening activity will help you to sleep well?

Then take into consideration *external* prime time. What is the ideal day of the week and time of day to conduct a certain activity from the point of view of the job market and other people? Here are some examples of prime time for many people working in a variety of companies.

- Do not call on a Monday.

- Try to contact a manager by phone late Friday afternoon.

- Work on job ad responses on the weekend so they are among the first to arrive, or work on job ad responses in the middle of the week so they arrive late in the screening process and stay fresh in the reviewer's mind.

- Suggest holding networking meetings the first thing in the morning, before or after lunch, or at the end of the day. Of course, fit into your contacts' desires.

- Interact with the personnel department just after lunch.

## Plan for Balanced Search Activities Example

|          | Monday          | Tuesday  | Wednesday            | Thursday | Friday   | Weekend    |
|----------|-----------------|----------|----------------------|----------|----------|------------|
| Early AM | Ad Response     | Research | Exercise             |          | Meeting  | Thank-you's |
| Late AM  |                 | Research | Letters              | Meeting  |          |            |
| Noon     |                 | Meeting  |                      |          |          |            |
| Early PM | Support Group   | Phoning  | Research             |          |          | Recreation |
| Late PM  |                 |          | Meeting              |          | Phoning  |            |
| Night    |                 |          | Friend/ Family Time  |          |          |            |

## Plan for Balanced Search Activities

|          | Monday | Tuesday | Wednesday | Thursday | Friday | Weekend |
|----------|--------|---------|-----------|----------|--------|---------|
| Early AM |        |         |           |          |        |         |
| Late AM  |        |         |           |          |        |         |
| Noon     |        |         |           |          |        |         |
| Early PM |        |         |           |          |        |         |
| Late PM  |        |         |           |          |        |         |
| Night    |        |         |           |          |        |         |

## *MAINTAINING CONTACT*

As previously mentioned, contact with people gets jobs. It's especially important to maintain contact with those you they have met during your exploring and niche-building networking sessions. At the time of the first meeting, you have only a small chance that they will know of a job opening. But over a year's period, your chances that someone in your circle will hear of a job that matches your interests significantly increase. Remember that, in networking, your brainstorming sessions generate new ideas, some of which come from the others. They have a vested interest in seeing them fulfilled. Your success in carrying out their suggestions will reflect positively on them; they want to see you succeed. So if they learn of something that connects with their ideas, they will remember it and pass it on to you.

Keeping in touch with a letter about once a month will keep you in their mind. Utilize the following:

- You might find an article or a Web site that fits one of their interests. Pass it on.

- You might have a clearer sense of career direction and might move from exploring to niche building. You would mail your new résumé.

- You might meet someone who knows your contact, and you have agreed to pass on some information about what they are doing.

Your progress letter can be transmitted either via land mail or email. In it, remind the person of your previous meeting, including a summary of what you discussed. Next, talk in a positive way about what you have been doing and what you have been learning. This letter need not deal only with you, and your contact will value your thoughtfulness and ability to remember details about him or her. Then get specific about what you are enclosing in the letter, talk about your plans, and reinforce your interest in keeping in touch.

In your letter, be positive about what you have been doing and the outlook for your progress. Here are the elements.

**Reminder and Summary.** Provide a sentence that will bring to mind your whole interaction.

"We met two months ago to discuss trends and possibilities in public health. Among the many ideas we discussed was that preventive health education will be receiving additional focus."

**Current News.** Let the person know what you have been doing and provide some current news the person will find interesting.

"Your suggestions were well founded. I have been able to meet with some people involved in marketing development for some HMOs, and it is, indeed, a source of significant future activity. One HMO has a project that began with a poll of physicians for ideas about how patient education aids could be improved."

**Specific Enclosure.** Take time to find something valuable to offer your contact.

"When we talked, I got the impression that you might be interested in how product information could double as teaching aids for doctors who use your products. I have enclosed one of the samples an HMO uses that was produced by one of its vendors."

**Future Plans.** Show that you are forward thinking, that you are going somewhere, and that you merit his or her investment of time.

"This area is of high interest for me, and I intend to meet people who are planning marketing campaigns for prevention."

**Communication Request.** State what you want, the reason for your writing the letter.

"Please let me know if you hear of any opportunities in any of my interest areas."

**Express Thanks.**

"Thank you for your help."

## PHONING

Look upon your phone as one of your most essential tools in your job search. You need it to follow up on letters you have written. You use it, often most effectively, for approaching hiring managers either with or without a referral. Also job seekers can call to ask if a job has been posted, a technique non-management and non-professional candidates found especially beneficial through job clubs. Their experience showed that, in smaller companies, quite a few job openings existed that never made it to the classifieds in newspapers or online. Participants had a high success rate in finding jobs in this way, and there is no valid reason why professionals cannot utilize the phone in the same manner as well.

When phoning for any reason, prepare to leave a message on voice mail. If you don't get a return call, repeat the process once.

**Phoning to Follow-up to a Letter**

Many of your letters will suggest how the other person can reach you, but reality says that for most letters you write you will need to follow up with a phone call. Here are the steps.

1. Ask if the person has received your letter and résumé.

2. If it has been received, ask if it is possible to meet.

3. If it hasn't been received, briefly introduce yourself and what you are doing, and ask if it's possible to meet.

4. If you get a negative response for a meeting, it could be because the person does not think it would be useful. Suggest that even a few minutes could be productive.

5. Suggest two time options.

6. If an in-person meeting isn't possible, ask if a short discussion over the phone is an option.

**Direct Contact to a Hiring Manager by Phone**

1. You may have the name of a manager from your networking or research. If you do not, call the main switchboard and ask to speak to the person in charge of the function that relates to you.

2. You are not asking for a job opening. You are asking for a discussion on topics about which you have advanced knowledge that the manager will value.

3. It's not usually helpful to over-do the pressure.

4. You may have an opportunity to follow up by sending an article or referring to a Web site.

5. You can refer the person to your online profile at LinkedIn.

## RESPONDING TO GREEN LIGHTS

As you talk with people and get referred to areas that are close to your next job, you may hear words like:

"That's a great idea." "We could use that." "I like that idea." "How would that work?"

Look upon these as invitations to become more specific about what a working relationship with you might be like. You might say something like:

"Could you be more specific about how we could work together on that?"

If you don't act to move towards a working arrangement, the other person may think that you are not ready or that you are not interested.

You have received keys to planning and persisting in a successful job search. These include ideas on balancing activities so that you remain energized, involved, and committed. You have also learned methods for maintaining contact, phoning, and responding to green lights.

- How did you get your last job?

- What improvement would you make to a prior job search? What would you do more of?

- Which of the modes of searching—physically walking around, reading and writing, interacting with people, and social networking—is your strength and which is your weakness?

## Chapter Twelve

# Memorable Interview

Your main goal in a job interview is to be remembered, and the best way to be remembered positively is to be seen as a person with unique interests and abilities. Adopting the competency philosophy will help you conduct an interview in which you will come across as a distinct and unique person whom others will remember.

The job interview, above all, involves human interactions, both formal discussions as well as other exchanges you may not consider part of the process. For instance, interviewers will notice—or eventually hear about—whether you care about the people you meet and how you respond to the "gatekeeper." The human qualities you bring to the table will affect them and strongly influence their opinion of you. They are looking for clues about how you will fit in the organization, how you will respond to managing, and whether you will contribute to the team in a positive way. The impression that you leave with the interviewer comes from not only the words you use but also your mannerisms, tone of voice, comfort level, and more. The logic of what you say contributes only part of the mixture. One way to attain the needed flow of vibes is to lock into the interviewer or panel of interviewers and move in coordination with them. Your words, responses, and questions will move in sync with theirs, and you will connect on other levels as well. The biggest win you can make in an interview is to be such a good listener and questioner that you identify one of their pressing problems and show how you would contribute to solving it.

When you are at your unique best, your physical, emotional, mental, and non-physical parts work together. What your body is doing, what emotions you are conveying, what you are saying, and what you are intending will work together for the superior results you want. Keep all in balance and focused on the same goal, and you will maximize your credibility.

Interacting and connecting between the interviewer and interviewee occur on the same four levels.

**Physical:** When two people are dancing together, their individual physical actions complement each other. One person moves the left foot forward, the partner moves the right foot backward, and this continues in a rhythm. In an interview, this is called mirroring and pacing. If the interviewer leans forward, the interviewee mirrors by leaning back, maintaining the space between the two of them. If the interviewer speaks deliberately, the interviewee copies the pace. The interviewee stays attuned to the other, just like in dancing, and moves accordingly.

**Emotional:** A connection on this level occurs when you indicate enthusiasm and excitement in your answer. This sends the message that you want to work there and sets a positive tone to the interview. Some anxiety is normal, and your interviewers expect that. Give an upbeat feeling, and you will make the emotional connection.

**Mental:** Answering completely the questions asked creates a solid mental connection. Both parties care that the content exchanged is accurate. The interviewer isn't just looking for an answer that works. He or she is listening carefully to identify the thinking process you are using and comparing it to what he or she is seeking.

**Non-physical:** This connection exists when both parties give information about each other's values. It's the deepest, and thus most binding, kind of connection.

## LEVEL THE PLAYING FIELD

As you enter the job interview, you need to feel you stand on equal footing with your interviewer so that the discussion proceeds as an exchange between professionals. A successful interview requires that you have the attitude and confidence of someone who belongs on the inside.

You also stand equal to the other people being interviewed. As with them, all of your work history and education have qualified you for the interview. As the interviewer places you on the spot to identify examples from your past, you need the confidence that what you say will equal or better the examples your competitors give. Others may have degrees and experiences that seem to put them at an advantage, but in the eyes of the selection committee, you have a combination of positive experiences, skills, education, personality, and more that make you not only unique but also worthy of consideration for the position. Maintain the confidence that, in coming across as the true and excellent unique you, your examples will be what they are looking for.

## RESPOND WITH EXPLANATORY EXAMPLES

An interview gives you the opportunity to show yourself as the kind of person who will succeed on the job. The use of examples and specifics enables you to show with your words and mannerisms how you acted in the past and how you will act in the future.

Plan to demonstrate your experience with the most important competencies for the job. Before the interview, identify those competencies. For example, a salesperson must be sensitive to the needs of the customer. Then select examples when you used them. Plan to use your examples to answer questions about your past. In preparing, pro-actively identify what you will say and the stories you will tell during the interview if given the chance.

When responding to open-ended questions, give more than surface answers. Go for depth. Surface answers cover the easy and obvious. For instance, in response to "Tell me about yourself," most people give a summary of their background—where they went to school, where they worked, what professional level they reached—all information available from their résumé. This doesn't paint a picture or tell a story that the interviewer will remember. A deep response, in contrast, makes a statement and then follows with an example or story that elaborates on and supports the statement. A deeper and memorable response to the above question would be, "One thing that makes me unique is that I always give everything I've got. For example, when I ski, I don't just stay on the trail. I go for the trees. I don't just downhill, I also telemark on cross country skis. I don't just talk about the interests of my client. I form a relationship with the other prosecutor, bond, and bring out cooperation. As a result, I had one of the highest percentages of reduction of sentence for my clients."

Avoid long answers. Their rambling nature indicates a lack of focus and impact. Instead, a good answer goes deep immediately. Around six sentences should satisfy most situations. Any more and the interviewee will likely only bore the interviewer.

## *BRING OUT ISSUES FROM THE INTERVIEWER*

The most impressive thing a person can do during an interview is to listen and draw out from the interviewer the current problems the company or department is having. In an ideal interview with a hiring manager, you should have a 50-50 exchange of information. To accomplish this, the interviewee needs to take every opportunity to get the interviewer talking. Based on your research about the company done before the interview or knowledge of the industry, have some good questions prepared and look for opportunities to use them. One way to do this is to attach a brief, relevant question to the end of interview answers, such as, "What in particular has been causing delays?"

# Preparation

When preparing for an interview, you should include practicing role-play situations to help you feel more comfortable in the actual interview as well as to have a good idea of how to respond to probable questions. Although interviewers will make every effort to put you at ease, it's normal to feel some nervousness or stress. Everyone does. Also, the interviewers might ask a few stressful questions. And when under stress, habits will play an even greater role in your response. Because the majority of one's performance stems from habit, you need to establish habits that will work to your benefit. Practicing in role-play situations allows you to change behavior habits and present yourself as the person you are becoming. Practice might include writing answers, reciting answers in front of a mirror, speaking answers into a tape recorder and listening to them, practicing using a video camera, or rehearsing with a friend.

Practice and use a technique to manage the expected stress during the actual interview. For instance, when asked a question, breathe and verbalize to yourself that you have a good answer. This is an example of how feeling some stress actually enhances performance.

## *Kinds of Interviews*

**Screening Interview.** Companies conduct this type of interview with you over the phone or in their human resources office. The company wants to insure that they understand your résumé and that you have the kinds of experiences required. Be prepared to explain in more detail your experiences at various jobs and what benefits you derived from them.

**Serial Interviews**. In the serial interview process, an applicant talks with a number of people, possibly in the course of a day. People down the line have been told which areas you covered adequately and which areas are still lacking in detail. Listen to the question and make an earnest effort to provide the additional information they want. A whole interview session might be spent on one area of your knowledge, interests, or abilities. The positive side of this type of interview is that you can more readily relax and act like your true self.

**Panel Interview.** Questions during a job interview are designed to bring forth all of your relevant actions. Identify beforehand the most important information the interviewer needs to know about you. When answering, pay attention to and give eye contact to the person who asks the question if the panel is alternating who is questioning. If the same person asks all of the questions, you still will need to attend to all of the people in the course of each of your answers. The goal of attaining a 50-50 percentage of talking is easier to attain in a panel interview.

**Hiring-manager Interview.** This is your opportunity to form a relationship with the person who will oversee your activities on the job and carry out your performance evaluations. Be personal and open. Make the same kinds of responses you make in the other interviews, but be more conversational and interactive about how you think you could influence a situation.

## SALARY NEGOTIATION

First of all, postpone discussion of salary until you have received a job offer. Discussing salary and other specifics before the company has committed to hiring you puts you at a disadvantage. Until the offer has been made, all of the power lies in the hands of the person able to offer a job or employment arrangement. Once a discussion like this begins, the other person may try to get you to offer your services for very little money, even for a free trial. If you have not received a specific offer, you might want to bend over backwards to cooperative and give in to a less-than fair arrangement. If your pursuit of the green light results in an invitation to move forward, and the person has asked you for a salary figure, you would first express your interest in the job and your positivity about the outcome of your discussion.

> "I really appreciate the opportunity to discuss working with an organization whose goals I share, and I am certain that we can arrange a fair working arrangement."

Saying this insures that you will not lose the opportunity. Then, move to elicit a definite offer.

"Until you specify the kind of commitment you are making to me, it's difficult to identify a salary figure."

You will next enter a sequence—put, pause, and propose—that may repeat a few times before coming to a satisfactory conclusion. Be patient, remain in control, and remember your end-goal of receiving an offer commensurate with your talents, experience, and potential.

**Put.** Put responsibility on the other person to make the first offer. Frequently, you might not understand the situation clearly enough to make an estimate of a good working arrangement. The other person knows much more. You might not have done enough research to know the right number.

"It's difficult to identify a figure without knowing the specifics of your company."

This is the first reason why they should make the first offer. The second reason is that it's a rule of negotiating that the person who talks first loses. That person has made his or her preferences known, has exposed a vulnerability, and will subsequently operate on the defensive. The person who waits has more flexibility and power.

**Pause.** Pause in response to an offer to indicate your thoughtfulness in this important matter. Ideally, the other person will make an offer. This could be a starting salary figure or a suggestion for a consulting arrangement. You can be certain that it is purposely low. The company plans to pay you more or provide a more favorable working arrangement. You can show perspective and power by pausing to show that you are thinking it over. The other person may also assume you think the offer too low, not worthy of an immediate response, and may make a higher offer.

**Propose.** Propose an alternative amount with justification. You need to have researched salaries and know the ranges in use because your response should be a range which includes the amount they will likely pay you. Most important, back it up with a reason that has value from the company's point of view, not yours alone.

"Given my ability to help you solve an important problem with no ramp-up time, I think that a figure in the area of … is more appropriate."

Continue the put, pause, and propose sequence. After you propose, you have put the ball into the other person's court. It's time for him or her to respond to make the next move.

## SAMPLE INTERVIEW ANSWERS

The major part of practically every interview follows the behavioral or situational methodology. You will be asked to identify a situation from your past and describe what you did in enough detail so that the interviewer can determine if you are the kind of person who typically takes the actions they are looking for. The theory is that people can be depended upon to act in the future the way they have acted in the past. To prepare, think of a large number of past situations that display your competencies, especially the ones the company is looking for, and practice giving answers. You can even write them out. Some of the negative situations in which you made mistakes will come into your memory. Always make the effort needed to think of a similar situation that was positive. Resolve to talk about the positive situation rather than the negative one.

Invariably, you will be asked to present some situations for which you cannot readily think of a good example. The pause here will be a little longer. You must think of the closest related example you can remember. Be totally honest. The beauty of this kind of interview is that you are genuinely connecting to who you really are. It comes across and is quite persuasive. But being totally honest does not mean that you need to talk about an example that will disqualify you. You can still decide to talk only about examples that will put you in a positive light for the job. Have plenty of example stories prepared in advance. 'Recognize that your competitors will have various experiences and will naturally choose to give only positive examples.

Use this three-step process when a question is asked:

1.  Pause and think to identify the one best answer and a supporting example.

2.  State your main point.

3.  Support what you say with an example. The same STARS format that we used to identify competencies can be used to tell a good story. A good six-sentence answer will include a statement, an example situation and task/challenge in it, three sentences describing the actions taken, and a result.

## QUESTIONS ABOUT YOURSELF

Prepare for these questions by increasing your self-understanding. This might involve making a short list of responses and prioritizing them. Then, say the priority response and give an example of it so that you provide a true, in-depth elaboration. Do not respond by just going over the list. The following questions will be asked in some way in every interview.

**Would you tell me about yourself?**

Do not rehash the history that's included on your résumé. If you get this question at the beginning of the interview, you will make the biggest impression by talking about what makes you unique regarding what you are driven to do in your next job. If you get the question towards the end of the interview, you might respond with information you haven't presented yet but which will spur the organization into hiring you.

> "What makes me unique is that I am passionate about what organizations can do to manage their public image. For example, I actively participate in our professional association. As an association leader, I put together the agenda for a conference that required me to contact leading experts in the field. I talked with many of them on the phone and learned quite a bit about their ideas. The result was a high participation level in the conference."

**What is one of your interests?**

This will probably surface early in the interview. The interviewer wants to know more about who you really are. Provide the deep view into your makeup that he or she is seeking. Say one priority, and provide an elaboration of it in a way that reveals who you are below the surface.

> "I am interested in group sports. For example, I play soccer once a week. For me, it's both social and competitive. The other players are serious about the game, but we all get along, and we have become friends. I think they especially appreciate my participation because I compliment people for good plays and always encourage everyone."

**What is one of your strengths?**

Provide a vivid and memorable example of yourself in action.

> "I am the kind of person who gets all of the facts, which certainly beats overlooking important details. For example, in getting the status report for a project, I asked my coworkers how they were doing. I was careful to ask follow-up questions, which allowed me to discover that the first answer they gave me usually left some false impressions. If I had assumed that those had been true, we would have finished behind schedule. But, we finished a difficult project within the timeline."

**What is one of your weaknesses?**

Interviewers want to know if you have the self-knowledge and openness to engage in productive performance discussions, so be real. Provide an example that shows a weakness but also gives it a positive spin by showing that you are successfully working to overcome this weakness. And, do not choose a weakness that will eliminate you from consideration.

> "Because I am very thorough, I need to insure that I also shift gears to see the big picture. In one meeting, I assured that I didn't get hung up on the details. I consciously stepped back to take in a fuller view, and ended up making a good high-level contribution."

### QUESTIONS ABOUT WHAT YOU HAVE DONE OR WOULD DO

Your answers to these questions allow the interviewers to picture you working in their company—competently or not—so your responses factor significantly in the decision about whether to hire you. In the competency methodology, companies have identified the actions of their above-average performers and grouped them into competency clusters. The "situational interview" format identifies whether you have the right cluster of competencies for performing at an equally high level. Interviewers ask for examples of past situations in which you displayed those actions and descriptions of how you would handle future situations. The interviewers have a checklist of what they are looking for, and when you act in a certain way in the interview or relate a story showing you acted that way in the past or give evidence you would act that way in the future, they check off that competency. However you will warrant a check only if you get specific in describing what you have done and why you have done it. In saying what you would do in the future, you need to provide equal detail and, in this way, demonstrate your thinking process. In preparing for these questions, think of a large number of successful past experiences that show you at your true and best self. This will help you when you need to think of examples quickly in the stressful interview situation.

**What is an example of when you tried to make an important point to others on your team or when you were promoting a program but were not successful?**

The key here is to think of the best example and stay true to what you actually did. Your voice conveys when you are talking from an actual experience.

> "People discounted the importance of the product modification I envisioned although I had an insight that it would make a big difference to the customer. When I saw that what I was doing was not working, I mocked up a demo and tested it with a customer. I relayed his reactions to the group, and with this bit of evidence, I got the okay for the product revisions, and the spectacular results amazed even me."

**What would you do if you had a difference of opinion with a workmate?**

With this question, there is a temptation to talk until you think you have it right. But you might end up talking too long, rambling, and losing your listener. You will give a better impression if you first pause, think, say what you would truly do, and end it with confidence.

> "I believe that differences of opinion often reflect differences of perception. I would get the other person talking about how he or she sees things. I would make sure to understand and verbalize what I was hearing. I would look for common ground in this discussion and use that in expressing a positive feeling that we could create the right solution if we worked together."

## QUESTIONS THAT TEST YOUR CONFIDENCE

Employers want employees that think, speak, and act with confidence. And they test your level of confidence by introducing stress into certain questions and noting your reaction. Your best preparation for this is to maintain a mental attitude that sees all questions as, first, an opportunity to show that you listen and communicate and, second, an opportunity to show how the successes from your past will make you a great employee.

In practicing these answers, you will also gain insight into the current status of your confidence and have the chance to improve it. Remember that these are stress-inducing questions and the interviewers have a correct answer that they want to hear.

**In summary, why should we hire you?**

This is your opportunity to think on your feet and show an understanding of the company's needs and your unique ability to fill them. The best answer will demonstrate an understanding of the situation that you have gleaned from the first part of the interview.

> "You have talked about your need for more comprehensive incorporation of customer information in product design. My experiences with survey research that I mentioned

earlier tie in to this. I also have an instinct for the next great idea. For example, at my last company, I anticipated one of our competitors' product changes, decreasing our response time. "

**What do you want to be doing five years from now?**

This seems like a question about your career and that you should talk about your dreams. But, more likely it looks for your current interest and focus as it relates to the organization. Interviewers want to hear that, after five years, you intend to have made a positive impact on the company and have advanced.

"I see myself contributing in a more significant way to an organization. For example, I am taking a workshop on business modeling. To get to a position in which I am influencing the whole organization, I am hoping that I will be able to work with different groups to gain an understanding of the variables they work with. At the same time, I will be forming relationships that will help me include variables that apply to the whole organization."

**How do you handle criticism? Give an example.**

When you hear this kind of question, immediately remind yourself that you do have a positive experience with handling criticism. Breathe deeply to relax and identify it. Then picture the example in your mind, see what was positive, and describe it.

"Receiving constructive criticism from someone with positive intentions always helps me. One example of when I learned something valuable was when my boss criticized me for not seeing the big picture about who I should talk with about plans for the coming year. At first, I felt at a loss, but then I figured out a smooth way to initiate the kind of contact that was needed. I asked my boss for feedback about the idea. She agreed, the needed planning was done, and I learned to think about my job with a bigger picture in mind."

**What is holding you back in your career?**

Everyone can identify events, people, poor decisions, or other situations that have held back his or her career. You may enjoy talking about regrets and what-ifs, but do not do it here! The correct answer is that the career decisions in the past have worked out, nothing has held you back in your career, nothing is holding you back now, and this job is the ideal next step for you.

> "My career has taken some interesting turns, and I have learned and benefited from each one. There is nothing that I would do differently. I took on additional responsibilities in my last job that have proven interesting and beneficial to me. I am looking forward to the experiences I will get in this job."

## CHAPTER THIRTEEN

# OVERCOMING OBSTACLES

Have you ever seen a baby crawling with abandon and touching everything in view to explore and learn? At one time you were that way, with high physical potential and no inhibitions limiting the use of your body. Emotions were flowing and fully expressed physically, and you were reaching out, touching, and discovering. You had no mental blocks, such as negative memories, impinging on plans. And, although you could not have voiced the idea, you had a feeling that your instincts were leading you to a great place. You had an intensity in physical, emotional, cognitive, and non-physical capacities. This potential to function fully in many kinds of activities is still within you, and you can take actions now to reclaim it.

Subsequent to your times of spontaneity as a young child, you have engaged in life events that may have dulled the glow and introduced a grain or more of doubt into the sense that you ares a winner. You may have failures and negative experiences—as do we all—and internalized them. As a result, capacities have diminished and your ability to solve problems has narrowed. The vision of your future career success may have faded.

# DEVELOPING CAPACITIES

You can work with each of your four capacity areas, identify how they are diminished, and reclaim your birthright potential. Everyone has traveled a path on which some capacities in each area have been fully developed. Others have been subdued for various reasons. Others have been ignored. The following suggestions for growing are designed to help you to identify your current stage of development and to provide some ideas for moving forward.

## *GROWING PHYSICALLY*

When you are sitting at your desk, looking for a good idea, what do you do? Possibly, you have gotten out of your chair, stretched your arms, rotated your body, and walked around. If the situation was stressing, you probably took some deep breaths and doubled the effort. If you were listening to your body, you could feel the energy within. And, often, a new idea came. Your physical side contributed to making something good happen.

Growing physically begins with movement and breathing. Just breathing deeply four times a day will increase the flow of oxygen to your cells, increase your energy and awareness, and result in improved functioning. Identify four different times when your schedule might provide a prompt. The first might be after you arrive at work and before you sit down. While standing, take a breath in which you expand your chest and lower your diaphragm to suck as much air as possible into the lower part of your lungs. Exhale just as fully. Other times might be after lunch, before you leave, and when you start your evening activity.

Other focused, physical activities can further enhance our performance in all aspects of our life, including at work and in looking for work. We haven't always had to think so much about bringing them into our daily schedule; we used to do it as a matter of course. In the beginning of our human history, our body played a much larger role in our functioning. Out of necessity, we had a higher awareness of our physical body and its influence on the rest of our personality. The benefits of moving and breathing were ingrained in daily living and taken for granted.

Over five thousand years ago, the simple movements used to improve health and human performance were recorded and systemized. Through experimenting and observing, theories evolved to explain the connection of movements to the flow of energy in the body that improved performance and well-being. The earliest was called qigong, which simply means using the impact of *qi*, or *chi*. Chi is the Chinese name for the life force that is recognized in every culture. It goes by many names, including energy, *elan vital*, *prana*, and grace. Subsequent experimentation and discovery included identifying meridians along which energy flowed and points that influenced the flow, knowledge which underpins the art and science of acupuncture today. Some breathing and stretching movements brought both physical conditioning and spiritual awareness, such as the practice of yoga. Other movements, such as tai chi, aikido, and karate, prepared a person for success in battle. The recently developed practice of Pilates uses breathing and movement to strengthen underused areas of the body to increase our physical awareness and improve the way our muscles are balanced.

A qigong session begins with simple movement activities that get the energy flowing. You can practice those initial movements and reap benefits throughout the day. Stand with feet shoulder-length apart and begin to move up and down at the knees, and then extend to moving all parts of the body in a shaking rhythm. Let all parts of your body move in all directions. The more movement you have, the more in touch with your physical resources you will be. Take full breaths. Then mentally go through your body and feel possible tensions in individual parts, and emphasize the movement of those parts in all directions: shoulders, chest, stomach, gut, hips, thighs, knees, ankles, etc. Feel as much of your body as possible. After a few minutes, stop and sense energy flowing. Then slap your body with an open palm front, back, and on the sides, from top to bottom, and back up again, repeating a few times. If you feel energized, you have become more physically aware of the flow of energy within.

To go further, recognize that everyone has knots of tension in the body that interrupts flow and communication between cells, organs, and systems. Breathing will help to break them down, but many will be too tight and will require body work beyond breathing. Eating a balanced diet of healthy whole foods and reducing poisons, such as alcohol, will help the body to rediscover its vibrancy.

Movement therapies such as Pilates and yoga combine stretching and breathing to connect mind and body. The eastern practice of qigong consists of simple movements that increase energy flow in the body and bring a strong feeling for self.

A relaxation technique called Progressive Muscle Relaxation (PMR) simply and powerfully reduces tension and begins to build physical capacity.[1] Sports teams use it to increase players' effectiveness because it moves their attention out of their head and into their body. You can easily carry out PMR. Handle any interference that arises in your mind during the session by simply letting it pass through. Here are the steps of a twenty-minute session.

1.  Create a mental space for this session by asking within for help in achieving the goal of relaxing groups of muscles and tissues.

2.  Begin by either lying on your back or sitting in a chair comfortably and upright and feeling both feet and seat. Breathe deeply to relax.

3.  Begin with the left foot. While breathing in, progressively tense all of the muscles of your left foot until they are tight, hold for a few seconds, and then while breathing out, progressively relax the whole foot. Breathe out further and relax further for the count of four. This can be combined with subtly feeling the movement of energy.

4.  Go through this breathing in and out, tightening and relaxing process with each body section: left foot, left ankle, left calf/shin, left knee, left thigh, left buttocks, right foot, right ankle, right calf/shin, right knee, right thigh, right buttocks, left fist, left wrist, left forearm, left elbow, left bicep, left shoulder rotator, right fist, right wrist, right forearm, right elbow, right bicep,

right shoulder rotator, pelvis/sacral, genitals/lower lumbar, gut/upper lumbar, stomach/lower spine, solar plexus/mid spine, lungs/mid spine, heart/mid-spine, esophagus/upper spine, shoulders, lower neck, voice box, mouth, brain stem, jaw, mouth/nose, cheeks, ears, eyes, forehead, brain, crown.

5.  Tense, hold, and relax your whole body. Scan your whole body from top to bottom. What is the most tense area? Listen to this part of your body and ask where the tension came from. A picture might come to mind. Picture times when you were using that part of your body effectively, and then picture a time when you will use it effectively in the future.

6.  End by giving thanks.

## GROWING EMOTIONALLY

Both genetic predisposition and experiences have a powerful influence on the ability to be aware of emotions and to act on them. Some people experience emotions strongly, have a vocabulary to name them, talk about them easily, and act appropriately on them. Others are less aware of their current emotions, lack the words to describe them, avoid talking about them, rarely express positive emotions, and sometimes express negative emotions inappropriately. Their past experiences may have involved feeling painful emotions and unconsciously deciding to block them out. This may have included tensing the parts of their body in which the emotions were felt.

To contribute positively to the whole self, the emotions—both negative and positive—need to be processed and resolved. Suppressing positive emotions hurts us as much as hiding the negative ones. If we are holding onto fear, we need to determine its source and take action to resolve the problem. If we have anger, we must express it appropriately and in a way that leads to productive action. If we feel love, we need to express it and let ourselves feel fulfilled. When we open the emotional pipeline, vibrations in the body rapidly convey what is happening and allow us to react in a way and at a time that work to our benefit.

If we feel threatened while in a well-functioning emotional state, we immediately notice the fear and prepare to escape or fight. If, instead, we feel safe and respected in the presence of another, we notice the possibility for friendship, and reach out in joy.

The pipeline can lose its effectiveness if we refrain from properly processing our emotions:

Some people ignore their emotions, and thus, they can neither share them with anyone nor talk about them. Unacknowledged but still very real, they lodge in the memory and body, reducing the capacity to feel subsequent emotions and hindering proper functioning of the other three aspects of the self. Remain aware of your emotions. Process negative ones by relaxing as they occur, reducing their impact. Naming and/or talking about them helps. By recognizing them, you prevent them from hiding and taking a toll on your body, mind, and spirit.

Emotions stay in memory and in the body. An emotional reaction may result not from the current situation but from a memory of the past that was similar in some way. Listen to your emotions, notice when they are not warranted in the current situation, look in your past to discover their cause, and resolve the past issue.

Good emotions require energy. Rest for reflection if you feel overwhelmed with too many good emotions.

You can improve the flow in your emotional pipeline and learn to manage all of your emotions by using this visualization process, which is frequently used by mind-body health practitioners.

1.  Sit in a comfortable way. Breathe deeply, and feel the air going to all parts of your body and relaxing them.

2.  Identify a negative feeling about a situation at work or somewhere else, and then locate it in a part of your body. Bundle it and move it to your heart area. Feel it in your heart.

3.  Identify a different situation in which you had strong good feelings, such as when viewing an inspiring scene at the end of an exhilarating hike, and locate where in the body that feeling is. Bundle that feeling, also, and move it into your heart, replacing the negative feeling so that it dissolves.

4.  Picture the initial situation and apply the good feeling in your heart to it.

5.  Breathe the good feeling through your heart, feel your heart expand, and picture yourself performing effectively.

Use this technique when you feel nervous about something or in preparation for an important event.

## GROWING INTELLECTUALLY

Your intellectual side can be a productive source for using knowledge effectively and solving problems accurately. It can verbalize an intention of what you want to happen. But it can also sabotage you.

Thoughts based on false premises can interfere in the analytical process and retard planning and performing. When we hold false ideas, they unnecessarily limit our career and other life activities. We all know people who have succeeded even though they were not like everyone else. And yet, we hold onto beliefs that those people should not succeed and others acting in a similar way never will. Some assumptions we might have learned and assume reflect the truth include:

- Large organizations have the best job opportunities.

- It's difficult to form the personal connections inside a business that result in a job.

- Shy people can't succeed in management.

- To help people you have to be in a helping profession.

- It's not possible to acquire the traits needed to succeed in a small business.

- To make money you have to follow what has worked in the past.

- Only fearless and highly talented people can start a company.

Sometimes these non-productive thoughts become loops of useless mental activity. We look for situations to support those ideas and ignore or downplay ones that counter our thoughts. By filtering what we pay attention to, we give credence to our false ideas, building them up until we no longer have room in our minds for another viewpoint on the matter. Our intellect gives us perfectly logical reasons to stay stuck in unfulfilling jobs or relationships.

But we can do better. We can control negative thinking and loops of negative thinking by becoming more aware of our thoughts and, once recognizing them, changing them.

In tough situations, fear can overwhelm logical thinking. Feeling stressed, we might exaggerate the negative, what Albert Ellis, the founder of Rational Emotive Therapy, called "awfulizing."[2] When confronted with a challenge, such as a difficult question on an exam, the thought, "There is no way I can figure this out in time, and I'm going to fail the test and fail this course," might burst into our mind. Giving in to such a thought will only prove it correct. Alternatively, we can learn to be aware of limiting thoughts and change them to something more accurate, such as, "This question will challenge me. I will have to work hard to get it right, but I have done it before, and I can do it again. This is only one question out of ten."

Handling negative thinking before it sidetracks you calls for knowing your ABCDs.

First, identify A—the Activating event, or the situation that gave rise to the negative thinking.

"A workmate acted in a cold way when I made some small talk."

Next, identify B—the thinking Behavior, or Belief, that you used to interpret the situation.

"That person does not like to talk about non-work activities."

Next, note C—the Consequence for your feeling or attitude.

"That person is not interested in a relationship beyond work matters."

And finally, D—Dispute the sequence with a new belief.

"I will assume that the person is having a bad day, and it's not about me."

Here is an example. You can also use this process to straighten out crooked thinking that has resulted from past negative experiences. For example, you may distrust authority figures. Using the ABCDs, you would identify A, what started this thought. Looking back, you might recall your first boss who yelled at you whenever you made a mistake. You would then see that you formed B, a generalized belief that resulted from that one event. Here, you might have concluded, "Bosses don't support me." Next, you would identify C, the result of this thinking, as your inability to have a positive relationship with managers. Future success at work depends on disputing this thinking and changing it to something productive, such as, "My boss supports me, wants me to succeed, and will be very patient. However, I need to approach her with good ideas and confidence."

Thinking becomes your ally when you use it to intend positive action in an affirmation. When you say what is true and what you want to be true, you set into motion a fulfillment process, acting upon what you believe. In this way, positive thinking can create a positive reality. "The profession I want to enter requires an ability to speak persuasively. I have the ability to learn this while still being true to whom I am, and I can see myself influencing people who appreciate my style."

## GROWING NON-PHYSICALLY OR SPIRITUALLY

We can improve our ability to use the power of spirit and vision towards our success in our career. Although we all have a connection with this non-physical reality and can draw upon it at any time, we tend to overlook and underrate it.

In the work world, harnessing our non-physical/spiritual capacity will bring about achievements on many levels:

- Achieving a more motivating vision as a leader of a team or an organization
- Inventing a new product or service
- Seeing a subtle trend that is key to a business strategy
- Anticipating a problem

- Persisting when discouragement stops everyone else
- Using intuition to identify a hidden reason for a success or failure

We see this capacity in ourselves and others when one person feels inspired while others in the same situation express boredom. That positive person is tapping into the spiritual connection, working with a personal vision, and letting it drive him or her to complete a given task, often oblivious to those stalled in the project.

We can all connect more fully with our non-physical/spiritual capacity and then draw upon its power to achieve our goals. Several methods can help us in this endeavor:

- Do you like to take a walk in the same place? As you enjoy its beauty or view or sounds or whatever physical aspect it holds for you, let yourself sense an internal connection through the physical to something much greater, more encompassing. Feel that positive connection and the power in it. Let an expanding confidence that something good can happen flow through you. Then, identify and picture what you want to happen.

- Access the power of the natural world. While walking in a place that you find especially beautiful, think of a problem you are trying to solve, possibly to improve a relationship or to chart a better direction for your career. As you walk, move your attention away from the problem and let a peacefulness fall within you. Create a blank slate, of sorts, in your mind, and as you continue to engage nature, be aware of the thoughts and messages that you are now getting as a result of making room for a solution. Move your focus to another view and notice when a different solution comes. Gather them and select the best one. Where did it come from? It began with a feeling similar to a hunch, and then it took on a non-physical reality within you, similar to a coach's vision for his or her team's victory.

- Begin meditation using a very simple approach. Set a goal of clearing your mind of all thoughts and accessing the power of the present. Assume a comfortable body position, either sitting in any way or lying down. It is not necessary to use the formal sitting meditation position, but do not get so comfortable, especially lying down, that you fall asleep. Close your eyes. Pay attention to your breathing as it slowly travels in and out. Breathe more deeply by moving your diaphragm down on the in-breath and up on the out-breath. Your stomach will rise and fall. As thoughts come into your mind, acknowledge them and ask them to pass through as you continue to focus on your breathing. Begin with one twenty-minute session per day.

- Adopt a practice involving stretching and breathing. Yoga and Pilates are two popular practices that are easy to begin. They result in increased physical awareness. Importantly, they also enhance a connection to the non-physical.

- Employ faith and persistence to bring about a positive change in your company. An important non-physical capacity, faith grows more powerful the more we use it; strengthen it through practice. Do something that is a stretch that you would not normally do and that requires faith. Monitor the results. For example, make a suggestion to a customer for an upgrade he or she would likely resist, or suggest a change in procedure that would make things more fun for you. And then have faith that your suggestion will generate the results you intend.

- Act on a hunch. All people have hunches, but many do not listen to or trust these messages.

## OVERCOMING CAREER OBSTACLES

As challenges arise, weaknesses are revealed. But we can handle any obstacle, overcome any weakness, thanks to the diverse strengths in our unique personality. Some bumps in the road may require time, some may call for learning and practice, some may need reaching out to others, but our self-assessment has shown us that we can succeed with perseverance. As we continue to surmount obstacles, we increase our self-knowledge, and our path towards work becomes more clear.

At this point in your work searching and career exploring, you may think that you are facing some obstacles. You may think that you have an inadequacy in one of the topics we have covered so far. This obstacle may be real or imagined.

- Power in a career comes from accumulating successful experiences. You have some, but do you believe you do? Even after our work in identifying and expanding past key experiences, you may think that you lack adequate experiences or marketable results.

- Success in a career requires a passionate interest in some aspect of it. You have at least one strong interest, but you may think you have failed to develop it adequately to mark your uniqueness.

- Job searching success requires connections with people, but you may think that you lack enough connections.

- Many jobs require a certain kind of education, and you may think that your academic preparation is inferior.

- Jobs may be scarce in your main areas of interest and ability.

- You may see an obstacle specific to your situation, such as the need to locate to an area not favorable to your career preparation.

Any change, such as the need to find a new job, challenges us, and we can view it as either a burden that holds us back or an opportunity that allows us to grow and adapt. A change involving our job and career has the potential to cut particularly deep through our personality structure. Casting aside what we have done thus far can feel like a rejection of how we have lived one of the most crucial parts of our life. We identify strongly with our work, so we may take this change personally, as if we are rejecting our self. But, it can also increase our self-knowledge and lead to new decisions that will start us down a path with a greater chance of success and reward.

Overcoming an obstacle of any kind requires that we see we can change something about ourselves to increase our odds of success. The first challenge, therefore, is to look at what we are feeling and what we are telling our self. This requires overcoming the natural tendency to deny some of the negative feelings associated with the current situation. Beneath the surface, we may have remorse over financial uncertainties or regret not having done something in the past that would have avoided today's painful circumstances. We might hold anger due to some kind of unfairness. If we keep these feelings unacknowledged, unrecognized, and unresolved, they may come out in some way and sabotage a career and job search. For example, fear associated with insufficient finances might keep us from taking any kind of a risk and lose out on a new but uncertain direction that perfectly matches our interests and desires.

When between jobs, we face managing a change that requires the engagement of our whole person. You have undertaken similar self-changes in the past with varying degrees of success. In an effort to improve yourself, have you tried to be more organized at work yet met only frustration? Have you tried to listen more and talk less in meetings and found your mouth has a will of its own? Have you wanted to take that first step in improving your career but always found excuses—all very good ones—to wait? The biggest reason why self-change efforts do not work is that they utilize only one of our capacities. Self-change efforts succeed when physical actions, emotions, thoughts, and non-physical connections work together in unison.

### Using All Capacities When Going through Change

*Jason entered the room on the first day of a career class in a state of visible agitation—his tight skin reflected his internal tension, he had nervous, involuntary twitching, and his eyes focused intensely on nothingness in space. When asked what he had been doing so far to help his career move forward, he responded that he had been making affirmations every morning, but they hadn't been working. Clearly, his affirmations were backfiring, making his situation worse and certainly not better*

*The cause of his affirmations not working may have been due to an over-reliance on his thinking side, letting his mind handle the situation. Logic would tell him that mere affirmations cannot change a situation and interfere with his absorption of the message. To get his mind out of the affirmations and let his non-physical side take over, he first needed to breathe deeply and identify how his situation was affecting his body. It would have been helpful for him to ask himself how he felt about his situation. He could also improve the power of his affirming by picturing feelings. When asked how he felt about some of his past career experiences it raised the possibility that some of those feelings were holding him back and needed to be addressed. During the class, we carried out breathing and relaxing activities, and Jason appeared to feel more awareness and control over his emotional state and power in his life.*

The physical, emotional, intellectual, and non-physical parts of us are connected. Our actions affect our feelings and thoughts, our feelings affect our actions and thoughts, and our thoughts affect our feelings and actions. And all affect our connections to the non-physical or spiritual. Any effort to change needs to address all four parts.

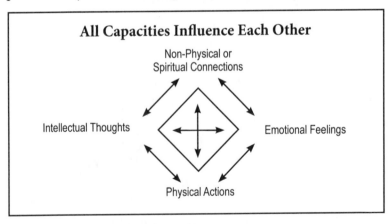

In the course of our life, we have taken on habits of actions, emotions, thoughts, and attitudes of having a purpose that limit us in various areas, including advancement in work finding. We want to identify those habits that have held us back and no longer serve us and then replace them with new behaviors that will allow us to move forward with success.

First, identify an area of concern—a negative experience from your past or a current way of acting or thinking that impedes your progress in some way. You might choose a minor incident, for instance, one in which you had lowered expectations for your performance on a job, or you might choose a mistake that put the brakes on your advancement.

Next, identify what you do or think that contributes to that area of concern. Consider at least one for each of your four capacities—physical actions, emotional feelings, intellectual thoughts, and non-physical or spiritual connections. These obstacles might concern an unhealthy view of money, not feeling worthy of attaining the ideal educational level, a low estimate of the professional contribution you will make, thoughts that you cannot find satisfaction in a variety of industries, or some other area in which you could be sabotaging yourself.

Finally, for each impeding entry you list, come up with a new way of acting or thinking that deals with the same issue but moves you forward. Those new behaviors will be the ones for you to practice and put into effect.

Here are three examples to help you get started.

## Area of Concern: <u>Denying the need to put adequate energy into a job search.</u>

| | Current Behavior | New Behavior |
|---|---|---|
| **Physical Actions** | Carrying out long-postponed interests to the detriment of the job search. | Treating the employment search as a job and identifying the best way to use time for a balanced life. |
| **Emotional Feelings** | Fear that rejection will be too tough to handle. | Handling this fear, as well as other emotions, appropriately. |
| **Intellectual Thoughts** | Verbalizing that I need to spend time on non-work interests. | Verbalizing that over the long term, I have been fortunate to have a balanced life, and that I will have that balance again, even though work searching is now a priority. |
| **Non-physical or Spiritual Connections** | Taking unusual action to control one's own destiny. | Awareness that life has presented this challenge, which will fit perfectly into my future picture. |

## Area of Concern: Not Reviewing Enough Options

|  | Current Behavior | New Behavior |
|---|---|---|
| Physical Actions | Making decisions without viewing the big picture. | Considering all relevant options in making a decision. |
| Emotional Feelings | Feeling worried about getting things in on time. | Feeling comfortable while reasonable researching options are carried out. |
| Intellectual Thoughts | Thinking that viewing more options will likely be too costly. | Verbalizing that individual perceptions are always narrow and that it's valuable to seek breakthrough ideas |
| Non-physical or Spiritual Connections | Awareness is totally taken up with observable reality. | Being connected to a large universe of possibilities. |

## Area of Concern: <u>Procrastination</u>

|  | **Current Behavior** | **New Behavior** |
|---|---|---|
| **Physical Actions** | Leaving things to the last minute and then doing them in an inadequate way. | Chunking challenges into doable bites and trying to do one step at a time. |
| **Emotional Feelings** | Fear of being inadequate in the activity. | Admitting that the fear exists and using visualization and breathing to resolve it. |
| **Intellectual Thoughts** | Verbalizing that it will take too long to do it correctly, and so I might as well rush it. | Verbalizing that it's better to do one small step well than to do more steps haphazardly. |
| **Non-physical or Spiritual Connections** | I know what will happen, and I will end up at the back of the line. | Believing that if you take a step with a positive expectation that good will happen. |

Select an area in which you might be sabotaging yourself and complete the following chart.

**Area of Concern:** _____

|  | **Current Behavior** | **New Behavior** |
|---|---|---|
| **Physical Actions** | | |
| **Emotional Feelings** | | |
| **Intellectual Thoughts** | | |
| **Non-physical or Spiritual Connections** | | |

- What is a past obstacle and where would you be if you had surmounted it?
- What is an obstacle you can control that is holding you back from your ideal future?
- Who can you ask about an obstacle that you cannot see?

## CHAPTER FOURTEEN

# BALANCE OVER STRESS

Finding meaningful work and accomplishing a work of art does not occur in isolation from other aspects of a person. It happens as a result of a life and personality that operate in balance. For example, one client who expressed concern over her career situation had another more pressing issue that held her attention. She was worried about not getting married and having a family, and she could not properly focus on understanding her career characteristics and presenting her competencies until some perspective and some problem-solving actions were brought to that issue. It was consuming her, and she had trouble making any career progress. Her life felt out of balance and so her whole being was wobbly. Once she understood her instincts more fully and could talk about them, progress on career issues could proceed.

You need to expend effort in areas other than work, or all of life's activities are jeopardized. Following are some of the areas that require attention. Identify a current or past activity in each of the areas, and then determine whether you have sufficient balance in your life.

**Life Balance**

| Friendships | Recreation or Sports | Community Involvement | Intellectual/ Spiritual Connection | Family/Root Connections |
|---|---|---|---|---|
| | | | | |

# MANAGING SPECIFIC STRESSORS

When we see a gap between what exists in our lives or in the world and what we would like to see, we want to make changes to fill that gap. But those changes invariably bring about stress. How much stress we will take on in closing such a gap depends upon several factors. If we believe that we have the necessary interests and abilities to handle the situation, our stress will be manageable. If the situation positively stimulates us, stress will only spur us on, and we will have the best chance of achieving our goal. However, if we see the goal as important but the gap too large for us to tackle, our stress will work against our efforts and may even overwhelm us so that we fall short of our goal. Ideally, then, we take actions to optimize our stress or at least make it manageable.

**Physical:** All stress affects our body in some way, so our stress management efforts should always include the physical body. For example, you can locate the tension in a specific place in your body, feel it, focus on it, breathe through it, and then picture it dissolving. Taking walks, exercising with breathing and stretching, getting sufficient sleep, and eating more healthfully all help your body reduce stress and keep it under your control.

**Emotional:** If you can identify what you feel in a stressful situation, you can use that information to change your emotions or work around them. Adopt a short-term strategy to get some immediate, affirming results, and also use a long-term strategy to deal with the stickier emotional issues at play. For example, you may notice that you avoid working on teams at work and, if you must contribute to one, you rarely speak up. Realizing that both positive and negative feelings about teamwork stem from interacting with neighbors and friends while growing up, you can focus on the positive memories so they replace the negative ones. For a short-term strategy, you could picture and experience in your mind the emotions from those instances in which you enjoyed participating on a team. For your long-term strategy, you could deal with the larger issue of self-acceptance in a personal development program.

**Intellectual:** What happens on the outside does not cause our stress. Only our reaction to the situation does. This means our thoughts control how we react and how we handle stress. Who controls our thoughts? We do. We can think different thoughts and keep stressful situations under our control. We can ask, "What am I telling myself to let this bother me?" Formulate an opposing message, and repeat the message in an affirmation. The office environment is a frequent cause of stress. For example, some people talk so loudly on the phone they seem to want to broadcast their ideas to the world. We can let ourselves feel irritated by the noise level, or we can change our thoughts about the loud voices and work despite the talking. The power to change—or not—remains with us. First, we need to identify our actual thought. It might be, "I need quiet to think clearly." You can use your intellectual capacity to manage stress by verbalizing an opposing message. You might say, "Although quiet is more comfortable to me, I haven't been exposed to consistent noise, and I might function even better in it." Your affirmation could be, "My neurons are positively stimulated by noise, and I am handling any problems with the breaks I take."

**Non-physical or Spiritual:** Ask, "What does this stress mean in the context of my life? What need does it fulfill? What can I learn from it? How is it a part of the excellent plan that guides my life?" For example, losing a sale can hold within it a valuable lesson on what to do differently next time to close a much more significant sale.

In every stressful situation, we can choose balance over stress by asking ourselves, "What is moving me out of balance, and what can I do to work towards balance?" Our client may be overly demanding of our time, our co-worker may be selfish, our managers may set a restrictive policy, or our work environment may be too cluttered. Typically, we cannot change any of that. But we can change how we react to the situation. We can take action using all of our resources.

For now, we can work proactively by anticipating how we will feel and think when under stress. Complete the following Stress Management Planning Chart to plan your responses to stresses in your environment at work.

### Stress Management Planning

| | Physical | Emotional | Intellectual | Non-physical or Spiritual |
|---|---|---|---|---|
| **Example:** Stress from a project deadline. | Stretch and breathe for 3-5 minutes every hour, or feel tension in the body and breathe through it. | Picture past successful project and feel increased confidence. | Change, "I have to use the same methods as others" to "I have options that can save time." | Value and appreciate this challenge and opportunity to be tested. |
| **Example:** A customer is angry. | Feel where the tension from the interaction is in my body and breathe through it. | Look for something funny about the person and laugh about it to myself. | Change, "I have done something wrong," to "I have experience with this kind of reaction. | Use what I learn to create a resource for other instances. |
| **Example:** A co-worker is asking too many favors without offering ideas. | Build awareness in my legs in preparation for standing up to the person. | Increase assertive feeling by picturing myself as a leader. | Change, "I can't say anything that might make waves," to "I can tactfully phrase what I say." | Overcome concern for self first by giving the person something. |
| **Your Example:** | | | | |

- What is a stressful moment from your past, and how did you handle it?

- What technique for dealing with stress works best for you?
- In your future exciting position, do you want more or less stress than you have now?

## CHAPTER FIFTEEN

# BUILDING
# NEW COMPETENCIES

What do you think is the most valuable asset you can have for succeeding in a career in a rapidly changing economy? It could be your education, but both the knowledge and problem-solving skills you acquired quickly become outdated. It could be the people you connected with in your education and related activities, but you are able to reach out to meet people and form a support network at any time. It could be your confidence in implementing job-finding strategies or entrepreneurial techniques that work, but your succeeding in the job itself matters far more.

Your most valuable asset for succeeding in a career is your ability to learn new knowledge and processes. That will enable you to stay current in work environments that are changing at an ever-increasing rate.

Your current job often offers the best place to grow and improve your potential. Learning activities you engage in there can be designed to improve both your current and future performance. You can receive accurate and constructive feedback from people who know you. Your current co-workers and managers probably know more about some of your best abilities than you do. They also know more about the weaknesses that most likely could hinder your future career success. And your current colleagues at work will engage in productive discussions about developing your competencies if you approach them properly.

In these changing times, you need to reinvent yourself periodically to reach your goals. You need to believe that you can change, grow, and develop. This involves being alert to the new competencies that the changing environments call for in your company and areas of interest. Picture yourself as a continual work in progress where you constantly present new, updated versions of yourself with added enhancements geared to a specific segment of the business world. Version 2 of a product is often much more successful than Version 1 because product development cannot initially anticipate all requirements in its targeted niche. Once the company launches Version 1, its developers listen to customers and monitor the product's use to determine how to improve it. The same holds true for developing your niche on your path to meaningful work. You put Version 1 of yourself out there and then stay alert for opportunities for improvement—and then act upon them.

## ATTITUDE TOWARDS LEARNING

Your reaction to this challenge depends on your previous educational experiences. If they have served you well, you will react positively to the idea of continually learning. If you feel either strongly or subtly negative about your past schooling endeavors, you may shy away from future efforts to develop yourself. It's important to identify, overcome, and reverse these negative feelings.

You may have had negative experiences in the classroom because of a clash between the primary way you learn and the primary teaching methodologies used by the teacher. You may have found classroom lectures boring and difficult to understand. Or you may have needed physical, hands-on activities to complete your learning and create a positive experience. You may get your best insights from talking with other people but were educated in classes that only allowed individual study. You may have succeeded in the theoretical discussions in the classroom but then failed to transfer the learning to real situations. If the kinds of learning you preferred or needed conflicted with the teaching methods used in your educational experiences, then you may have a negative attitude towards learning. Regardless of your negative experiences, changing your ideas about learning into positive ones will enhance your ability to learn now.

Everyone has engaged in successful learning experiences in his or her past, but those experiences may not have been in a traditional classroom, and so we may discount our ability to learn new ideas or practices. According to Allen Tough, adult education researcher and professor from the University of Toronto, 95 percent of people participate in significant learning each year. Also, 70 percent of learning experiences are self-directed and outside of formal educational settings.[1] In these experiences, you, the learner, identify a priority, set goals, and recruit learning resources. You may have learned a hobby such as gardening, learned how to take care of a pet, learned how to use a new product, learned how to operate software, set up a piece of furniture, investigated a country for travel, discussed a book, or learned a language. Learning is already exciting for all of us, but we need to realize it.

Use the following worksheet to match some positive past learning experiences with different learning methods and then decide what to do with those methods now—whether to utilize, develop, or avoid them. The left side lists a large number of learning methods, divided into the four capacities: physical, emotional, intellectual, and non-physical. When considering your activities that represent using each method, be sure to include all of your learning experiences and not just those from the classroom.

### Positive Learning Activities

Think of a past activity for each learning method listed on the chart on the next page Identify those you prefer and wish to continue to use, those you would like to develop further, and those you would like to avoid.

| Learning Methods | Past Activity | U-Utilize or D-Develop A-Avoid |
|---|---|---|
| **Physical**: Learning by experiencing, doing, and practicing.<br>• Practicing, making mistakes, and receiving constructive feedback<br>• Using your senses in learning, such as reciting what you are learning out loud<br>• Using your hands in drawing or coloring, building physical models<br>• Manipulating physical models<br>• Using music and rhyme to memorize information<br>• Playing a sport | | |
| **Emotional:** Learning by listening/watching/ teaching others, feeling the acceptance of another person.<br>• Discussing in a group and seeing things from different perspectives<br>• Teaching and explaining a task or concept to others in words they can understand<br>• Creating a drama in which emotions are acted out<br>• Being assertive in a debate | | |

| Learning Methods | Past Activity | U-Utilize or D-Develop A-Avoid |
|---|---|---|
| **Intellectual**: Learning by analyzing and seeing relationships.<br>• Taking time by yourself to see the logic and relationships of the topic<br>• Memorizing processes<br>• Committing new ideas to memory<br>• Drawing a picture<br>• Making a list, contrasting and comparing, drawing a flow chart<br>• Thinking on your feet in a debate<br>• Making a comparison of theme | | |
| **Non-physical**: Learning by understanding deeply, seeing new intuitive connections.<br>• Meditating on a concept<br>• Creating a mind map showing the big picture and relationships<br>• Developing a story<br>• Identifying symbols<br>• Creating an expressive work of art | | |

Recalling positive learning memories establishes a solid investment in your future. You will know the kind of learning to seek. And knowing the rate at which you learn, you can plan when to start and how much lead-time to allow for acquiring targeted skills.

- Which learning methods do you associate with favorable learning experiences and want to utilize now?

- Which are not as natural for you but you know you will benefit from developing them?

- Which do you resist and would prefer to avoid? Recognize that in reaching your goal of becoming a balanced, whole person, you may need to engage in activities you would rather avoid. So, your lack of interest might indicate a road sign for future development.

## SELECTING LEARNING GOALS

Learning can be divided into two categories: education and training.

The word "education" comes from the Latin words "ex," meaning "out," and "ducere," meaning "to lead." Together they mean to lead out, which happens when you engage in activities that will bring out, help you to understand, and to take the next step in the evolution of all of your career characteristics: values, intelligences, tendencies, interests, and abilities. Education makes you a better person in all ways and happens at all stages of your life, not just during the formal schooling years and not just in a formal school setting. You find the experience intrinsically worthwhile and seek out opportunities to improve your whole self through various educational means.

Training, on the other hand, prepares you for something specific. It could be learning to perform an aspect of your job more effectively or preparing to do something new on your job. It could be improving your skill in a sport or other hobby activity. Training increases your effectiveness in a specific situation.

Some learning activities may involve both education and training.

There is a hierarchy of training goals if you are currently in a successful employment situation. Your hierarchy depends on your individual situation. Here is a suggestion for a priority order that applies to a large number of people, with Number 1 as the most important.

1. **Developing a competency that helps you perform more effectively in your current job.** Humans can satisfactorily

learn a wide range of competencies for most situations. Go several steps beyond "satisfactory" in your current work, and you will make the most valuable contribution possible to your career. Your increased effectiveness will receive recognition from others, and your self-esteem will grow.

2. **Developing your personal capacities so that they are in better balance.** You will realize increased effectiveness in everything you do, and you will experience less destructive stress. If a person is high in intellectual capacity but low in emotional capacity, he or she will have great ideas but not the kind of interpersonal relationships to use them effectively. If a person inhabits the non-physical world too much over the physical world, his or her ideas will not move from possibility to actuality.

3. **Developing a competency that is in a current area of strength, has the potential to be developed further, and will help in the accomplishment of a valued goal.** This will enable you to make a contribution which is significant to both you and others. And it will make your work feel meaningful to you.

4. **Developing a weak area that might hold you back from being effective in using your priority competencies.** No one likes to look at his or her weak areas. Spending time there usually drains energy. Find a way to balance developing your strengths with bolstering weak areas so you can perform at a higher level.

Examining the status of the competencies you are currently using on your job or will use on your next job can help you identify areas needing development, which leads directly to your setting goals for learning. The left side of the following chart demonstrates how to examine your competencies. It looks at a competency, organizational savvy, on three levels of performance—high, medium, and low. For that competency, some of the person's actions associated with it indicate a low level of competence, some a middle level, and others a high level.

Examples of how a person could perform at low, medium, and high levels for the competency of organizational savvy are listed.

To identify your current position on the competency dimension called organizational savvy, think of a past related experience story and select an action that is typical of your performance regarding organizational savvy. Then look at the actions that anchor the dimension. Compare the typical action you have selected from your past story to the action for each level. Locate your current level of competence on this three-point scale, low, medium, or high. If you remember talking with people in a different part of the organization about what you were doing but did not try to engage their motivations in your project, you are in the middle. One of your learning goals can be to learn how to engage others to help with your projects. Your learning will help you to increase your standing on the organizational savvy competency dimension.

The right side of the chart provides an opportunity for you to identify your status for a competency which will play a role in your future. Select a competency that you know will be important and write it in the top open box. Next imagine three kinds of behaviors, low, medium, and high. Write them in the boxes at the bottom, middle, and top of the dimension line. Then think back on your experiences when you were using that competency. What was one of your typical actions, and where on the competency dimension does it fall? Write it in the box at the corresponding level.

## Competency Dimension Chart

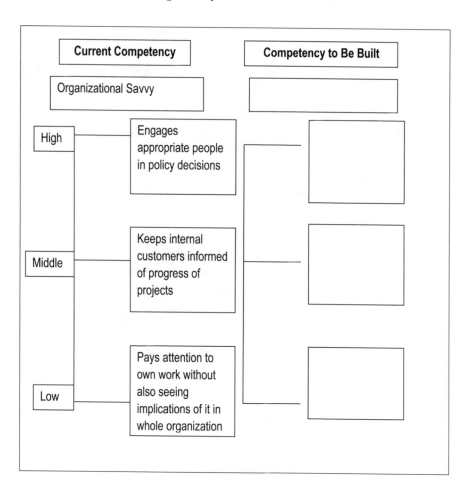

As you explore your niche, you will learn about excellent performance and see some areas you would like to develop. Your learning goal can be to move to a higher level on one of the competencies that is important for your meaningful career future.

- Did your prior learning accomplish its goals?
- How can you improve your planning for learning?
- What learning goal is most important for you now?

# PLANNING FOR EDUCATION AND TRAINING

In the past decade alone, our society has seen a tremendous increase in information handled in the workplace and knowledge needed for effective performance. Institutions of all kinds have arisen to fill the increased need for training to help people cope with and capitalize on the overwhelming complexity. Many offer solutions for special logistical needs, such as closeness to work, variable time schedules, intense short-term activity, and spread-out activity to fit into a busy schedule. The Internet has provided an answer to many of these concerns by enabling distance learning and promises only to increase the variety of subjects and formats available.

Education and training are considered competency-based when they teach what you need to do to be a success. It goes beyond presenting only knowledge to presenting all of the elements of effective actions to insure that learners use knowledge effectively. This kind of learning includes hands-on or experiential elements, going beyond mere lecture and presentation.

Learning from all sources now receives respect from businesses that know their success depends, first, upon performance and that may or may not tie into employees having degrees from prestigious institutions. Employers use selection methods that quickly get beyond impressive labels to identify true competence and accept many sources of education and training as valid. Workshops, conferences, certificate programs, and self-study provide effective methods for individuals to increase their competence and marketability. Often, such methods reflect greater initiative in the individual who must create an appropriate learning package than a degree program that has all the parts already in place.

Learning can also be totally self-directed. Utilizing a competency-based method is especially effective when you are on your own. You can identify a specific action in a specific situation you need to learn and recruit a partner to provide feedback and mentoring.

When managing your own learning, adapt these steps to suit the kind of learning which is best for your learning capacities and the situation. Select a learning activity which matches your goal. If you are working on being more effective in meetings, don't just read about it. Practice responding with the right action in a specific situation. If you need to use graphics more effectively, don't just practice using graphics software. Find some situations that need something graphical to make a point more effectively, and practice thinking of as well as producing something creative.

1.  Select a competency to develop.

2.  Identify a person who will provide knowledgeable feedback and mentoring in that competency and negotiate a schedule and possibly financial consideration.

3.  Identify a behavior within that competency you would like to develop.

4.  Select a situation in which you can practice and then demonstrate expertise in that behavior in that competency.

5.  Research and read to obtain information you need for carrying out the action.

6.  Take action. Nothing happens by only thinking about it.

7.  Have a healthy attitude towards mistakes. See them in a positive light—mistakes provide you with clues about where you need to improve. And realize that they are a sign you are extending beyond your comfort zone, that they show you are progressing. Reacting negatively to a mistake only works against you.

8.  Engage in feedback and mentoring sessions.

9.  Steadily increase the difficulty level of the situation until you achieve your desired level of expertise.

10. Reward yourself.

## FORMAL EDUCATION AND TRAINING PROGRAMS

Will a formal degree or certificate program help? Typically yes. A respected and accredited learning organization has focused its energies on a career niche. You will learn about the latest ideas from experts in the field. You will engage your whole being because you will be sitting in a classroom, working in groups, and discussing ideas with others. You will be inspired to become a new and more effective person. You become part of a community of learning with alumni.

Is a new degree or certificate required? It depends. You can do all of the above on your own or as an intern in an organization. You can research a niche and engage in all kinds of learning experiences. You can seek out people for discussions. In the process of obtaining an internship, you will meet useful people of all kinds. Many employers have developed their unique way of doing things and don't like their new hires having first to unlearn what they learned in a school. The fact that you are doing this on your own may also impress management.

Continual learning is now an essential element in finding your work and completing your work of art. Learning options have expanded dramatically so that one or more match your unique learning characteristics.

- What is an example of when you engaged in self-directed learning in the past, and how did it work?

- From what you know about yourself now, what is a possible future occupational role and what kind of learning will help you get there?

- Will you need a new degree, or will another learning experience provide adequate results?

## CHAPTER SIXTEEN

# INTEGRATING TO
# IMPROVE PERFORMANCE

You have engaged in self-understanding activities that will deeply motivate you to contribute your abilities to creating a result that you value. You have learned presentation and interacting skills that will help you to connect with opportunity more effectively. You have seen how to take advantage of opportunities for personal growth. Now, to perform your work of art, you need to see how you can improve your performance.

The major cause of a failure is usually not inadequate ability or lack of intelligence but neglecting to attend to an aspect of the problem. For example, salespeople most likely lose a sale not for lack of ability or training or attributes of the product. Instead, they likely fail to follow a sequence of prescribed steps for a successful sale. They may have neglected to mention an important fact about the product, forgotten to address an emotional need, overlooked a logical advantage, failed to explore enough options, or felt doubt instead of confidence at a crucial point in the sale. In order to include all problem-solving steps appropriate to the situation, you need to follow a problem-solving model.

Traditional advice for improving performance usually recommends that you follow a series of steps. A sequence such as the following is often recommended.

1.  Identify the real problem.

2.  Generate a diverse set of alternatives.

3.  Evaluate these alternatives in terms of advantages and disadvantages.

4.  Select one alternative and create a plan of action.

5.  Take action and monitor results for probable modification.

However, these steps need to incorporate what we have learned about utilizing one's whole self in any endeavor for maximum effectiveness. For instance, identifying the real problem requires that we consider emotions as well as facts, that we see cause-and-effect relationships, and that we intuit what is under the surface. Seeing alternatives requires out-of-the-box thinking that those who access the non-physical and artistic capacities often implement. Selecting the best alternative requires both analysis and hunch. Planning requires estimating future possibilities. We need to use a problem-solving sequence that points out the importance of thinking in different ways and that helps us to pay attention to using all of our parts: physical, emotional, intellectual, and non-physical or spiritual.

Besides helping you deal with the problem under consideration, using the enhanced problem-solving steps suggested here will help you to move beyond habits that are currently hindering your performance. This method will give you better results than you have achieved in the past and will help you look at current challenges with fresh eyes.

The Integrated Performance Model leads you through steps so that you will use the resources of your whole person to achieve success. It raises your awareness of when information and energy are moving into you from the problem situation and out of you to form the solution. It differentiates between the physical and non-physical aspects of a problem and insures that you consider both. It contains separate steps for feeling/emotional processing and logical/mental processing and insures that you consider both.

The first four steps involve attending to what is coming into you from the situation:

**Experiencing** signifies sensing—moving all the physical energy and information from the situation into the self. Fully absorb and appreciate everything in the situation. Your senses are attuned and open to all sights, sounds, textures, and smells. You may kinesthetically feel the depth, height, and width of all of the physical elements.

**Reacting** signifies feeling—moving the emotional energy and information from the situation into the self. Emotions directly connect your well-being with the situation. If there is a reason for you to pull back or to be attracted, you will get a signal to do so. Effective problem solving demands that you are aware of the signals you are receiving and take actions to handle them properly. With this connection, you appreciate the emotional dynamics in the situation.

**Assessing** signifies thinking—moving the mental energy and information from the situation into the self. Your thinking enables you to see cause-and-effect relationships and to solve problems in the most efficient way possible. Analyze what you see to identify the key ideas, hypothesize, and then experiment to identify a cause and effect. Develop opinions about what is working and not working.

**Understanding** signifies intuiting—moving the non-physical energy and information from the situation into the self. You can see beyond cause-and-effect relationships and arrive at a deeper insight about the way things work. To accomplish this, you need to use both analytical and synergistic thinking. This provides a wise perspective and an understanding of possibilities. It brings a large number of options for the way ideas can be connected.

The second four steps involve attending to what is going from you back into the situation as your answer to the challenge:

**Envisioning** signifies intuiting—moving the non-physical energy and information from your self out into the world. You imagine an ideal and create a vision of something that is possible. This involves associating one idea with another and optimizing so that you see the best outcome from a large number of possibilities. Humans have the unique ability to envision something that is not there and create change.

**Intending** signifies thinking—moving the mental energy and information from your self out into the world. Believe in a vision and then commit to it in your mind with conviction. More people fail at this point than any other. Your belief must withstand the doubts of any around you as well as any you harbor. To bring it closer to reality, verbalize what you believe will happen. Stating what you believe goes beyond affirmations. It confirms your certainty in the outcome.

**Expressing** signifies feeling—moving the emotional energy and information from your self out into the world. Send energy when you are carrying out your actions. The effectiveness of your performance depends on the energetic vibrations you bring to your challenge. You can express this in its highest form as a controlled intensity and focus.

**Embodying** signifies sensing—moving the physical energy and information from your self out into the world. All of your attention focuses on your body performing in the situation. In this state, everything you do flows through your body in a more effective way. When your body is fully expressing your vision and intention, it acts like a finely tuned instrument, producing a true work of art.

You can use this model in a visualization process to prepare for an event or to solve a problem more effectively.

### Integrated Effectiveness Visualization

1. Sit comfortably and take a relaxing breath in and out. Picture yourself sitting in front of a stage, watching yourself and all of the characters and physical elements of one of your performance situations.

2. Picture and absorb the scene in all of its physicality and sensual input.

3. What are the feelings in the scene? What are the other players feeling? What are you-on-the-stage feeling? Let you-the-viewer feel those emotions. Say something to yourself to handle it. Breathe a relaxing breath through the negative feelings.

4. Assess the situation. Who knows what? What key causal point, if addressed, will lead to a solution?

5.  What are all of the possibilities of what could happen both positively and negatively? Feel the power in the situation and the complexity.

6.  What is your intuition about this activity? Do you deserve to succeed? Feel totally aligned with your purpose in life in solving the problem at hand.

7.  Envision the good outcome you would like.

8.  Intend and verbalize to yourself what you are doing to create a positive outcome.

9.  Attach an enabling emotion to the picture, and express that emotion.

10. In mental rehearsal, picture the events unfolding. What is the initial challenge? See yourself responding. What is another challenge? What are you doing? Who is helping you? Take the next step. See yourself breathing in the situation and out the answer.

11. Step back and view yourself deploying all capacities and functioning fully.

12. Now, thank yourself for its creativity. Feel appreciation for who you are and what you did. Slowly move your body and bring your attention back to your seat.

These steps have been derived from what we do every day to solve problems. The visualization will enable us to do it more effectively.

- From what you know about your personality, which of these steps will be easiest to implement and which most difficult?

- Think of an example from your past when you performed at a low level. What could you have improved using the Integrated Performance Model? What different results might you, then, have achieved?

- What is an area in which it can help now?

CHAPTER SEVENTEEN

# HEARING A CALL

Notable writers, entertainers, and business people have attributed their success to listening. They are referring to more than paying attention to the words someone else has spoken. In addition, they have moved from a self-centered view to an attitude in which their total focus was on others' needs and on what needed to be done in the world.

In *Work Finding*, the initial emphasis is on self-discovery and self-development. We looked to our past to identify key stories and learn about our values, needs, intelligences, preferences, interests, environmental support desires, and abilities. We learned to communicate our career assets effectively. Then we changed focus to what is happening in the workplace and where we might fit. We researched to expand our perceptions. In walking around, we consciously observed. In responding to published jobs, we studied employers' needs and matched the stories in our letters of interest to them. In networking, we asked leading questions and then listened, acknowledged, and reinforced what others were saying through their words and intentions. We learned to speak in job interviews to show that we will meet the employers' challenges. We observed what we could improve in our search for work and overcame obstacles. We noticed the competencies that we needed in our target work areas and pursued development activities.

Now we are looking for a call. The best way to insure that we hear one is to improve our listening, which includes focusing more strongly on workplace needs and challenges.

What will the call sound like to you? What is it's language? Following are four examples. The first person, Steve, emphasizes responding to and overcoming immediate challenges. The second person, Anne, pays attention to messages from people first. The third person, John, seeks to learn from the logic of the situation. The fourth, Elizabeth, first tries to understand the bigger picture. If these people were lost in the woods, Steve would forge forward, clearing brush if needed. Anne would talk about what to do with the others in her group because appreciating different perspectives is a big help. John's first instinct would look for clues, such as were the moss on the trees is, to bring a logical solution to the problem. Elizabeth wants to see the big picture. She might climb the highest tree and look around.

We are all unique, and our career progress takes different forms. Which is similar to yours?

*Steve had a successful corporate career which culminated in leadership in succession planning. He began in the operations planning part of the company, and as he accomplished major tasks, greater options arose. Without knowing his exact career path, he stayed true to doing what he wanted, what he enjoyed, and developed skills that, almost magically, fit perfectly for the next move. Without conscious effort, the way always remained open and clear to him. He said he felt as if he had known from an early age what he was supposed to do. He gave more attention to listening and responding to immediate opportunities than long-range planning. And because he remained in tune with his inner desires relating to work, and because he kept his eyes open for opportunity, he naturally followed his path.*

*Anne naturally connected with people, and the purpose of every career move was to find additional ways to do that. She moved from teaching to food sales, and then to recruiting. When she was relating, she was happy and effective. Her progress was fuelled by her friendships with others. To develop other parts of herself, she listened to the feedback she was getting from others and pursued additional education in business leadership, educational leadership, and educational policy. Networking was a natural extension of what she loved to do. Based on the relationships she formed in her internship experience and the knowledge gained from her education, she obtained a job in school administration.*

*As an engineer, John was a natural planner. He enjoyed and benefited from all of the career activities in our program, beginning with the stories and ending with interview answers. His networking followed the pattern of discovering options, building a niche, and consultant marketing. With no friends in town and with the no-frills interpersonal manner of an engineer, he met with over fifty people, developing options in publishing, education, construction customer service, and maintenance supervision. He won a highly sought-after maintenance supervision position for a county because of his hard work in looking at himself, learning about what was happening, seeing options, prioritizing, and making logical choices.*

*Elizabeth pursued new directions, moving from business operations, to business communications, and then to writing children's stories. She felt the risk but had a feeling that she was on the right path. She could not identify in advance the exact next steps but had faith that some viable options would arise when needed. She was able to find part-time work as an editor. To increase her success in marketing her stories, she built competencies in marketing and speaking and gave presentations in schools. Because fortunate and unexpected things did happen, she felt that there was a plan for her life. Her focus was on future possibilities.*

Many of the activities in *Work Finding* are designed to help us understand which part of our personality is dominant and which might account for our blind spots. Steve sees the world from a **physical** perspective. All of his resources are focused on living practically in the present. Anne's dominant part is the emotional side. The primary driver of her career decisions is how she can be connected to additional people. John's **intellectual** side plays the major role. He seeks to identify the cause-and-effect relationships that will lead him to the best decision. In making her career decisions, Elizabeth places her attention on the **spiritual or non-physical** parts of life. She trusts her hunches to lead her in the right direction and limits the use of factual data.

Over and over again, we have emphasized that we each have a unique self that grows in power as we better understand it, build its capacities, and use what it has to offer in a positive way. Our self has expanded because physically we have flow rather than tensions, emotionally we have passion, intellectually we have accurate beliefs, and spiritually we have optimism. The more we stay true to our unique self, the greater the success we will find—on the job, in our interpersonal interactions, in work finding, and ultimately in discovering our calling. Do you identify with one of these four ways of managing your career? Do you have an insight into your dominant part? This understanding is crucial for clearly feeling your priorities.

All of the people in these stories heard a call. It may have felt like an attraction or a pull. They might have heard the message in reflecting on a networking meeting that went particularly well. They might have pictured themselves engaged in an activity and feeling more joy than they have experienced in their past work. They might have succeeded in initiating a contact that indicated opportunities were opening up. Or, they might have found a group of people forming around a new idea where they fit in.

A common thread in hearing a call is "extreme listening." Extreme listening involves more than keeping an open ear to words spoken. It also requires asking perceptive questions, which get other people talking about ideas or events that concern us. It demands taking lots of notes during networking sessions, reading them just after the meeting and adding more information or insights while the interaction remains fresh in the mind, and then reading them again at a later time. It means standing back to get a new perspective and then connecting the dots to reveal the pattern. It calls for carrying around a notepad and writing down all of the good ideas that are popping up in our mind. When we practice extreme listening, we leave ourselves receptive to hearing our message. And when we receive it, we get a new view of power, one that extends to all outside of us and connects to our inner self. Our power and potential grow as we open our perceptions and our personality, and we feel a connection to something greater than ourselves.

The steps of finding work in *Work Finding* are similar to those that we might take in walking a labyrinth of circular paths, culminating in a center of power, similar to the one on the cover of this book. Walking around the outside, we review both our positive and negative experiences. As we progress along the inner paths, we ask what in our personal makeup gave rise to those experiences. As our self-understanding deepens, we see that our personality is made up of parts and they can be developed to build a bigger self and balanced to build a more effective self. At the center, we experience a heightened self, one that is connected to a source of power. With inspiration, we walk back towards the outside with a more confident self. As we approach the outer rings, we see new and interesting challenges and engage more effectively in all areas of our life. And we know that to improve our life we can walk the labyrinth again and that, when we do, we will find at the center a more mature self that is connected to a source of power in a more effective way.

We know the path we need to follow to satisfy our deepest desires, to reach fulfillment in this life, to contribute to the world in the way only we can. We understand our whole self—the one that has succeeded and failed at numerable endeavors, worked to improve, and changed direction as a result. And we know where to proceed, if only we will listen. Although a message arises from within, we sense a pulling from the outside, a voice from without. Our deepest desires and motivations lie before us, waiting for us to take action. Looking back, do you see that there has always been a plan for you? Look for your own feelings and thoughts about being driven towards something. Look beyond where they are hiding. They are in all of us.

The decisions we make to move from an ending place to a new situation forms our path. We need to listen to its messages and follow the calling. When we step in the right direction, we connect to a higher self, see many more possibilities, and become inspired to give. We obtain knowledge, understanding, and wisdom that will enable us to see relationships and meet people that facilitate change in the world. We contribute ideas that fill a need that brings an increased sense of meaning. We take steps towards bringing something non-physical into physical being through visualization, verbalization, emotional expression, and actualization. We package our vision in a language that others can understand, and by naming it, enable a project to move beyond our narrowness and take on a life of its own.

We might get only hints about the message that we're receiving, sometimes crouched in the most unlikely places. A peak experience in which we were so fully engaged that we found a time of bliss might hold a clue to where to proceed. Supposed good luck might indicate more than mere happenstance. A time of failure might hold a key to success.

The drive to follow a direction will not come from a logical decision-making process only. Our newfound conviction comes from acting with and listening with our whole being. When we turn up the intensity and get involved in enough situations, something special will happen. We will feel in sync with our self, feel right about what we are doing, and feel we have arrived at the place we have sought for so long. After all of our traveling, we have come home.

# Appendix I
# Ten Coach or Counselor Steps for Facilitating Competency Based Interests and Abilities Discovery

**I**nsure **Appreciation of Range of Career Assets.** Begin by talking about when it's important to be aware of one's career assets, such as when making a career decision, asking for a raise, or looking for work. Discuss some examples of assets, such as using a saw, being accurate, giving good customer service, thinking thoroughly, having foresight, and expressing empathy. The competency methodology does not distinguish between personality strengths, tool/process/book knowledge, personality characteristics, or technical understanding. All might be competencies, and all are transferable.

**Bring Out and Combat Obstacles to Self-understanding.** Ask about obstacles to getting on board with this. Examples are a history of poor performance in school, fear of insufficient or inadequate assets, and lack of confidence. These are sometimes seen in fake bravado.

**Bring Out the Person's Career Path of Experiences.** Point out that the word "career" comes from the word for "carriage path," and then ask what makes a good path. For example, a successful path provides increasing rewards in some way, such as monetary compensation, recognition, responsibility, or knowledge. For a productive path identification, it's important to include experiences from hobbies, social interactions, volunteer experiences, and community involvements as well as past jobs.

**Lead Recollection and Suggest Additional Experiences.** Most people resist looking back because what comes up first is often a failure. A coach or counselor tactfully assists in navigating over or around these. He or she is able to notice unrecognized areas of interest and suggest that the client look for certain kinds of specific experiences. For example, people with natural empathy may not see that strength area as something with career potential because they are so close to it and take it for granted. They could be asked to write about a time when they helped a friend. Or, others may have successes in investigating, but may not recognize it. They could be asked to think of a time when they solved a problem using thorough investigation.

**Expand Key Experiences.** Introduce STARS stories - Situation, Task or Challenge, Actions, Results, and Strengths Themes. Ask for an example experience, and demonstrate the questioning, suggesting, and eliciting process that results in the discovery of actions indicating potential competencies. Competencies are those actions which combine the person's priority values, intelligences, preferences, interests, etc. Use the STARS worksheets to expand seven experiences, the number that all career counselors agree brings out needed breadth and depth.

**Reflect, Enlighten, and Encourage.** Individuals do not have the objectivity to identify all of the actions they have taken and the good things they have done in the key experiences in their career. The coach or counselor needs to listen, acknowledge, encourage, suggest themes, and lead in order to bring out additional important information. Both client and coach need to brainstorm what the individual may have been doing that indicates possible competency. Help the client to appreciate how unique he or she is based on the way in which the person met the challenges written about in the STARS stories

**Cluster Competencies.** One of the keys to freeing oneself for career growth is to move beyond past labels. Instead of a client's thinking of one's self as a project manager, he or she needs to see a person who anticipates problems, understands the strengths of team members, and moves towards results. If one or more of these actions are a competency, they will be seen in one's other experiences. The clustering process will bring together similar kinds of actions and create motivation for using them. Begin by listing all of the actions in all of the experiences that were expanded. Select one action that is most motivating. Look for other similar actions and make a grouping. Then, identify the next most motivating action which is not in a group. Cluster similar ungrouped actions around it. Move actions around if needed. Continue until there are six to ten competency groups. Then look at the actions in each group and identify a competency name.

**Prioritize Competencies.**. Use a pair-wise comparison grid to compare each competency with every other. Ask the person to imagine him- or herself using the competency in a specific situation and identify the intensity of the positive feelings. Record a vote for the competency with the strongest positive feeling. As a coach or counselor, question to bring out why the person is making some of the selections. The person will gain an appreciation of how head and heart come together to choose a priority.

**Practice Communicating with Examples.** Too many people present themselves with lists of words therefore, do not make a strong impression. A perfect solution exists in the competency methodology. A competency is stated and followed up with a specific example story. It's the story which most effectively conveys career potential.

**Expand Perceptions.** A client's stories enable a friend or someone in a business or other employment situation to see possibilities for using their competencies in work settings. The perceptions of the client are expanded when he or she hears these new options from another person. In the role of a coach or counselor, demonstrate how, when a person presents him- or herself in a specific and unique way, options for new opportunity can be identified.

# References

## Chapter 1

1. William Bridges, *Job Shift* (Reading, Massachusetts: Addison-Wesley, 1994), 62.
2. Tom Jackson, *Guerilla Tactics in the New Job Market* (New York: Bantam Books, 1991), 3.
3. Daniel H. Pink, *A Whole New Mind* (New York: Penguin Group, 2005), 51.

## Chapter 2

1. Richard Nelson Bolles, *What Color Is Your Parachute-2008?* (Berkeley, California: Ten Speed Press, 2008), 241.
2. Calvin S. Hall and Vernon J. Nordby, *A Primer of Jungian Psychology*(New York: New American Library, 1973), 96.
3. Howard Figler and Richard Bolles, *The Career Counselor's Handbook* (Berkeley, California: Ten Speed Press, 1999),58.
4. Figler and Bolles, ibid, 77.
5. Richard Nelson Bolles, *What Color is Your Parachute-2010?* (Berkeley, California: Ten Speed Press, 2010), 177
6. Jerald R. Forster, Ph.D., Articulating Strengths Together (Center for Dependable Strengths, 2009).

## Chapter 3

1. Abraham Maslow, *Towards a Psychology of Being* (New York: John Wiley and Sons, 1968).
2. Howard Gardner, *Frames of Mind* (New York: Basic Books, 1994).
3. http://www.newhorizons.org/strategies/mi/dickinson_mi.html
4. Donna Dunning, *What's Your Type of Career* (Palo Alto: Davies Black Publishing, 2001), 10.
5. John Holland, *Making Vocational Choices* (Lutz, Florida: Psychological Assessment Resources, 1997).

## Chapter 4

1. David Bubois and William Rothwell, *Competency Based Human Resource Management* (Palo Alto: Davies-Black Publishing, 2004), 17.
2. Lyle Spencer and Signe Spencer, *Competence at Work* (New York: John Wiley and Sons, 1993).

## Chapter 6

1. Nancy Cook, "Blue-Collar Blues" (*Newsweek*, May 17, 2010).
2. http://www.bls.gov/emp/ep_table_102.htm
3. Catherine Rampell, "Recession Cuts Some Jobs for Good" (*Seattle Times*, May 13, 2010), 10.
4. http://www.bls.gov/emp/ep_table_103.pdf
5. http://www.bls.gov/opub/mlr/2009/11/art4full.pdf

## Chapter 10

1. Jane Finkle, "Social Media: The Revolution in Career Development" (NCDA Career Convergence, May 3, 2010).
2. Stephanie Booth, "How to Find a Job," *Real Simple* (June, 2010).

## Chapter 11

1. Richard Nelson Bolles, *What Color Is Your Parachute-2008?* (Berkeley, California: Ten Speed Press, 2008), 11.

## Chapter 13

1. Eugene Gendlin, PhD, *Focusing* (New York: Bantam New Age Book, 1981).
2. Albert Ellis and Catharine McLaren, *Rational Emotive Behavior Therapy* (Atascadero, California: Impact Publishers, 2005).

## Chapter 15

1. Allan Tough, interview by Robert Donaghy, 2005, http://ieti.org/tough/learning/donaghy.pdf

# ABOUT THE AUTHOR

Bill Gregory has worked for over thirty years as a career counselor in higher education and outplacement settings. He originated the use of the acronym STAR to help people identify and talk about their accomplishments. He was a co-founder and President of the Puget Sound Career Development Association, and has been active in presenting conferences for both career professionals and job seekers such as Windows of Opportunity. As a program manager for a major online career portal, he designed offerings and recruited and managed partners. His organizational experiences include performance management, identifying competencies, and evaluating training methods. As a counselor he has utilized mind-body techniques, such as focusing and bio-energetics. He has an EdD in Higher Education from the University of Washington, an MEd in Guidance and Counseling from Seattle University, an MBA from Amos Tuck, Dartmouth, and a BA in English from Holy Cross.

Bill is currently bringing together thought leaders to present Work Finding Webinars, which provide advanced topics to help those in transition who already have excellent résumés, have completed job interview training, and need to do something additional. Go to www.workfinding.com to see the times for Webinars. Topics include:

- Defy the Economy

- The Inner Work of Work
- Feeling Your Creative Spirit
- Clear Obstacles with Your Authentic Power
- Acquire a Survivor Personality
- Leverage Your Uniqueness

The Work Finding.com web site also contains a listing of career coaches and counselors who can help you develop the inner resources you need to move forward and who can open your eyes and help you use new ways to network and uncover opportunity.